ENDORSEMENTS

★ *Every page of HEATKTE - Michael's and Sheryl's personal account of how they have turned a huge personal challenge into a springboard for achievement - became an inspiring wake-up call for me that reminded me of two very important things: 1) Appreciate what you have every day and, 2) Life's challenges are wonderful opportunities for personal growth.*

Doug Lipp, Former Head of Training at Disney University, Author of Disney U.

★ *Michael & Sheryl Bergdahl have written an excellent book full of practical ideas to inspire you and improve your life. Their premise is simple but powerful: high expectations are the key to everything. Raise your expectations by applying what the Bergdahl's teach, and you will enjoy increased personal success.*

Mark Sanborn, Best Selling Author of The Fred Factor, Former President, National Speakers Association

★ *A touching, inspiring personal story that reminds us all of what's most important in life, and challenges us to take responsibility for living our highest purpose. Treat yourself to a great read. I highly recommend it!*

Scott Friedman, CSP, Former President, National Speakers Association

★ *HEATKTE is one of the most refreshingly useful compilations of the essential drivers of success to come along in years. All those who read Michael and Sheryl Bergdahl's book will be inspired to reach higher and work harder to achieve the life of their dreams.*

Robert B Tucker, President, The Innovation Resource Group

What readers had to say about HEATKTE

This is a book that will be of value to everyone, from an executive behind a mahogany desk to a teenager on a school bus. The message of authentic personal empowerment is delivered via compelling, inspiring, and deeply moving personal examples from the Bergdahls' own lives, presented with a straightforward integrity and honesty that is irresistible. The HEATKTE principles lay out a clear roadmap to the life to which we all aspire - a life of purpose, success, and joy. I wholeheartedly recommend this book to everyone!

Ruth Ann, President, Information Technology Company

Overcoming life's obstacles is crucial to achieving one's goals, and Michael & Sheryl Bergdahl have artfully and inspirationally explained how to do so. HEATKTE is truly an enjoyable read for anyone who desires to live with passion and purpose.

Patty, Small Business Owner / Entrepreneur

Michael and Sheryl's book HEATKTE is very inspirational. I especially enjoyed the personal stories. I struggle myself with weight loss and I am going to finally get this weight off with the inspiration from this book. Thank you for showing me that when you believe and work hard to achieve a goal, anything can happen!

Ellen, American Sign Language Interpreter

Michael & Sheryl provide deep insights into how to succeed in both your personal and working life. This book will lead you down the path to positive thinking with amazing real life stories that are guaranteed to help open new doors for you. HEATKTE will be the most life-changing book you have ever read!

Mario, Business Development Officer

HEATKTE is a book that will inspire you to pursue your personal and professional dreams, regardless of your age. By combining the ingredients of high expectations with a positive "can do and won't quit" attitude, passion, integrity, and courage, you have the recipe for achieving personal and professional happiness, and success in your life!

Koren, National Sales Director

HEATKTE- High Expectations Are The Key To Everything holds the answers to recognizing and realizing one's full potential. This is a life-changing book!

Roberta Joan, BSN, Registered Nurse

Michael and Sheryl have been on an amazing journey to overcome many challenges. I avoid the word "adversity" because to hear Michael and Sheryl tell their story there is only joy and acceptance of the many bumps in the road. They have been raising a family, building a business, and best of all, gaining passion as a couple while tackling their disabilities and life challenges head-on! They are an inspiration to couples and parents in how to achieve balance.

Pam, Business Owner

Filled with inspiration and wisdom, this is a book everyone will benefit from reading. Michael and Sheryl Bergdahl open their hearts to us, passionately sharing their own personal experiences in an enduring, powerful message, challenging us to adopt guiding principles and convictions which will both direct and motivate, as we face all manner of life's challenges. In HEATKTE, the Bergdahl's remind us how to truly define "success", and give us a path to achieve it! A MUST-READ for everyone!

Joseph, Manufacturing Company President

A well written synthesis of what it takes to succeed in life. The Bergdahl's strive with their 6 principles to exhort us all to do better. I agree that preparation and perseverance are the twin keys to succeeding in life.

Walter, Hard of Hearing Teacher of the Deaf

HEATKTE is a must read for anyone working towards self-improvement and personal growth. The message is beautiful: through clear visualization, positive affirmation, and perseverance, it is possible to meet expectations set upon oneself, even with unexpected circumstances.

Katie, School Teacher

"Everybody's got something" is an understatement after reading this inspirational book. Yes, we all get frustrated and have challenges, but most of us never know what it is like to face obstacles that totally change your life. You can choose to just "give up" or you can be grateful for what you "can do". This book will motivate and change your outlook towards yourself and others. A must read.

Mickie, Former Non-Profit Executive

If you find yourself struggling to succeed, then this is the book for you. It is full of insight and inspiration that will put you on the road to success.

Carol, Retail Management

DISCLAIMER

Although this book is designed to provide accurate and authoritative information with regard to the subject matter covered, Michael & Sheryl Bergdahl, the authors, make no representations and give no warranties or guarantees with respect to the accuracy or completeness of the information. The contents of this book are not intended as direct advice, recommendation or counsel, and we do not intend for you to rely upon it when making, or refraining from making, any career or life decision. The information is provided for informational and entertainment purposes only. If you are considering making a major life or career changing decision, and you feel you are not qualified or experienced enough to make that judgment, you should seek professional advice before acting. The information in this book is of a general nature and you should not consider it specific advice for your unique circumstances. The opinions expressed in this book are those of the authors only, and as such you should not consider or take the information as professional counseling or personal advice for your career and life, or as a substitute for qualified one-on-one career, life or legal counseling.

High Expectations Are The Key To Everything

H.E.A.T.K.T.E.

Michael Bergdahl

With Ideas, Insights & Inspiration from
Sheryl Bergdahl

Foreword by Mark Sanborn
Best Selling Author of *The Fred Factor*

Published by Motivational Press, Inc.
7777 N Wickham Rd, # 12-247
Melbourne, FL 32940
www.MotivationalPress.com

ISBN: 978-1-62865-080-8

Contents

**To Heather & Paul,
Our Daughter and Son:**

*Discover, accept, and embrace the wisdom
contained in these fourteen 2 letter words,
and you will always control your own destiny:*

*If it is to be . . .
It is up to me . . .
To go do it!*

FOREWORD

I am honored to write the foreword for this book. Michael and I first met in person while speaking at the same conference for a client. I was immediately impressed with his ideas and the way he delivered his message.

Michael is a deep thinker who can draw powerful insights from what he's done and observed. He has written books about Walmart and Sam Walton, two huge success stories in their own right. In this book, High Expectations Are The Key To Everything (H.E.A.T.K.T.E.), he makes it very personal. You'll gain insights from the challenges that confronted Michael and his wife Sheryl (the inspiration for this book). Best of all, you'll learn a perspective and specific practices that can help you deal with your own challenges and make the most of your opportunities.

I agree with Michael about the power of expectations. The truth is most people don't expect much because they don't want to be disappointed. I believe the greatest disappointment of all is living life beneath your capabilities; of never pursuing your potential.

We are better people when we expect more of ourselves. And we help others become better when we expect more of them. Think about it. Aren't you better for the positive expectations of your parents, coaches, mentors and friends?

HEATKTE will give you an advanced degree in how to benefit from high expectations. Michael communicates these great ideas with clarity and conciseness. Consider what he recommends in the pages ahead and do what he suggests.

With themes like striving to reach your full potential, seeking a mentor, learning from the success of others, getting out of your comfort zone, and being willing to take calculated risks, I wholeheartedly endorse what

HEATKTE teaches. In this age of easy answers and quick fixes, Michael respects and cares enough for you, the reader, to tell you the truth about what it takes to triumph over circumstances and succeed.

It is one thing to know how to do business well but quite another to truly know how to live well. Michael and Sheryl are those extraordinary individuals who understand both, and they make excellent guides for you in this book.

Your destiny awaits!

Mark Sanborn, Best Selling Author of *The Fred Factor*
Former President, National Speakers Association

HEATKTE
(Pronounced: Het-**Ka**-Tee)

*This book isn't about how to bring out the best in others;
it's about how to bring out the best in you!*

INTRODUCTION

High Expectations Are The Key To Everything

Always striving to do your best may be challenging, but the effort itself enhances the satisfaction you feel when you ultimately succeed!

The lives of every member of our family changed in an instant on July 7, 2003, at three o'clock in the morning. That was when my wife, Sheryl, to whom I had been married for 27 years, was afflicted by a catastrophic ischemic stroke which severely injured her brain. She was taken by ambulance to a nearby hospital and I remember standing in the emergency room, and later in the intensive care unit, contemplating *why this had happened to us?* Sheryl was only 48 years old at the time, and I thought strokes only afflicted older people; not active *young* people like her.

As I leaned against the wall outside the intensive care unit, I experienced for the first time in my life that feeling of being completely alone; that feeling of being uncomfortable in my own skin. My mind was flooded with thoughts, feelings and emotions as my mind raced out of control as I reminisced about all that Sheryl had meant to our family. Panicky, I started thinking irrational and negative thoughts about the future. The harsh reality of the situation shook my confidence and stole my emotional strength. I was certain the comfortable life we had known had ended forever and been replaced by a challenging, difficult, and obstacle strewn road ahead. I was already thinking about selling our two-story home in order to buy a more manageable one-story house, so we could take care of Sheryl more easily. I prepared myself for the worst, and to be honest, I had extremely low expectations; the future just looked so bleak. Standing there alone in the hospital hallway, I silently prayed for a divine intervention.

It took about 10 days in the ICU before the doctor would let Sheryl awaken from her medically induced coma. Those were the longest days of our lives. The big concern at that point was the extent of her brain injury. While in the coma, the doctors had no way of diagnosing the impact the stroke had on Sheryl's intellect, memory, personality, speech, let alone her physical capabilities. In the days that followed, we received some very bad news. Sheryl's stroke had caused permanent paralysis to the right side of her body; her right arm, hand, and leg were now permanently paralyzed. The news was particularly devastating, because Sheryl was right-handed.

At the same time the doctor also gave us some good news. Though the location of Sheryl's stroke had caused permanent damage to her right side, she had not lost any of her mental faculties. We were thankful she had retained her memory; she still had her sense of humor and she had a positive attitude. Though she was by no means conversationally fluent, she could carry on a short coherent conversation. Despite all of the problems we would now face, surprisingly, she and I experienced wondrous joy at the fact that she had not only survived the stroke, but that her indomitable spirit was still alive and well! Now, the biggest immediate concern she faced was whether or not she would ever be able to walk again.

I visited Sheryl in the hospital every day with gladness in my heart. Our family was blessed because she had survived and she was now on the road to recovery. She was a bit groggy and tired easily, but in one of our first good conversations we talked about the future. I told her how I was having trouble focusing, and that I felt ill-equipped to balance the management of all of the household chores, looking after the needs of our two children, while simultaneously bringing home a paycheck. Given our circumstances, I asked her what we should do and I'll never forget the calm direction she gave, lying there in her hospital bed. *I know what I'm going to do. For the next 6 weeks, I will remain in this hospital recovering from my stroke. I'll be receiving physical therapy treatments seven days a week, trying to learn to walk again. While I'm here, you need to take care of our children, manage the household chores, and pay the bills.* When she put it that way, the challenges I faced seemed much less daunting in comparison. My immediate problem was that I had low expectations, my confidence was shaken, and I was wallowing in my own self-pity. In that instant her calm advice changed everything. I finally realized I had to proactively assume the role of "*Mr. Mom*" and take care of our two children, help with homework, buy the groceries, cook the meals, wash the dishes, do the laundry, pay the bills and earn a living! *As I thought about it, single parents face similar challenges every day without complaining, so why couldn't I do the same by trying to temporarily fill Sheryl's shoes?* Today, as I look back, I feel a bit embarrassed by how cowardly and selfishly I had acted.

Sheryl's reaction to her stroke was truly inspirational, and in fact her response, and my response, became defining moments in our lives. We learned that the challenges we faced, and that our family continues to face, are not, and never were, insurmountable. When we first experienced adversity, I reacted as many people do by assuming I was not equal to the challenge; I had extremely low expectations. Fortunately, Sheryl provided the inspiration I needed when I had lost faith in my own ability to deal with the life-changing challenges in front of us. She led by her own example by continuing to set her goals high as she simultaneously re-motivated me to do the same. Together, we discovered the importance of remaining positive when facing overwhelming challenges by making the best of a bad situation.

We also discovered life teaches valuable lessons that can only be learned by facing adversity. Remarkably, we learned that life tests you first, and only later do you discover the important, powerful and sometimes life-changing lessons. That's exactly what happened to us. From living through these difficult experiences we learned valuable lessons about our own family's character, our tenacity and our ability to adjust to rapidly changing circumstances out of our control. Our family proved that ordinary people can find the inner strength to endure and continue to prosper when facing overwhelming odds. Amazingly, Sheryl's stroke brought our family closer together. It is for this reason we now view what happened to Sheryl as our *stroke of luck*; for our family it turned out to be *a blessing in disguise*!

This book is somewhat autobiographical in nature as it includes insights from our life experiences and those of our family. We will explain how we embraced *"high expectations"* to overcome adversity and still achieve career and family goals. Michael's observations are based on his perspective as a Christian business leader. He has included experiences from his more than 25 years of Human Resources background, working with diverse groups of people across six different industries. Sheryl's insights are based on her experiences as a teacher and mother.

The personal stories we have shared are designed to help you avoid some of the mistakes we made along the way. We have woven into our writing the most important lessons we've learned about overcoming adversity, triumphing over tragedy, and achieving our dreams. Our observations are also based on my interactions with people in our travels around the world. The lessons included are in reality a lifetime collection of wisdom from the real world experiences of both of us; Sheryl's as a parent, wife, homemaker, nature lover, international traveler, and stroke survivor; Michael's as a father, husband, outdoorsman, caregiver and storyteller.

The pages that follow are often written in the first person due to the fact that having a singular voice is said to lend clarity to a book. That's a bit misleading, because this book is the by-product of both of our lives, and this is as much Sheryl's book as it is mine. It was a team effort, and I hope readers will remain cognizant of that fact. You will discover that this book is a series of true stories that could not have been written without her ideas, insights, and inspiration.

When we started writing, Sheryl and I simply wanted to share the life lessons, good and bad, we had learned the hard way, with our daughter Heather and our son Paul, who are now young adults. Our goal was to capture the knowledge and experience we had learned from the school of hard knocks, and the school of life experiences, in hopes of making their transitions in life a little easier. A secondary, yet equally important goal was for us to leave a legacy for future generations of our family members. As the writing unfolded, our goal broadened as we wrote with the intent of helping all aspiring young people, high school and college students, entrepreneurs, business people, those with disabilities, those experiencing career frustrations, or anyone else facing seemingly insurmountable obstacles. This book is designed to help them and you to better understand how to overcome life's challenges, take control of your own destiny, and most importantly, how to achieve greater success and happiness in life. Fortunately, you'll learn you already possess the power, know-how, and all the tools you need!

The lesson that serves as the overriding theme for this book is *High Expectations Are The Key To Everything*. It made all the difference in our lives, and we hope it can be the catalyst you are looking for to make a difference in yours. *Your HEATKTE Journey begins now!*

Michael & Sheryl Bergdahl

HEATKTE
(Pronounced: Het-**Ka**-Tee)
Key to Success #1

High Expectations Are The Key To Everything

HEATKTE Keys to Success

KEY #1: VISION & PURPOSE

KEY #2: PLAN & STRATEGIZE

KEY #3: EFFORT & EXECUTION

KEY#4: AFFIRM & BELIEVE

KEY#5: ACHIEVE & SOAR

KEY#6: PERSEVERE & OVERCOME

HEATKTE Key to Success #1

VISION & PURPOSE

> I know if I have drive, ambition, and am willing to work hard,
> there is little doubt I will achieve my dreams!

Many years ago, I learned a motivational secret used at one of the world's largest companies to inspire average people to perform at above average levels. They called this performance motivation technique *"HEATKTE"* (pronounced Het-**Ka**-Tee) which they said is a pseudo-American Indian word. HEATKTE was a manager-led ritual utilized at the beginning of employee meetings to drive home the importance of achieving high standards. There was a HEATKTE song and a HEATKTE dance; lead by a manager playing an American Indian tom-tom drumbeat, BOOM-boom-boom-boom, BOOM-boom-boom-boom, BOOM-boom-boom-boom! Well, you get the idea. The point of the HEATKTE ritual was to create a fun focal point to promote the importance of continuous improvement, continuous learning, and striving for excellence.

Communicated to managers, supervisors, and employees alike, HEATKTE created a self-fulfilling prophecy. You see; H.E.A.T.K.T.E. is an acronym that stands for High Expectations Are The Key To Everything. The intent of the song and dance ritual was to focus every individual on the importance of achieving the company's lofty performance standards. The not-so-subtle implied message was that anything less than giving your very best effort would be viewed as unacceptable. Interestingly enough, the HEATKTE ritual actually worked!

From that experience, I learned that high expectations are the key to everything I wanted to accomplish in my life, and I really believe it's the same for your life too! When I say everything, I mean everything. Having high expectations in your life isn't just the key to achieving success in some things, many things, or a lot of things. It is the key to achieving success in everything! The good news for each of us is the decision to prosper at the highest levels is a matter of personal choice. You see, you can make a decision today to become the very best, and if you stick with that commitment, that's exactly what you will become. If you live your life embracing the HEATKTE philosophy, you can't help but create your own self-fulfilling prophecy for personal success!

A good example of how having high expectations makes a difference in people's lives is the story of Dave, who works at the local post office where we live. Every time I walk into that building Dave greets me by name, and he takes time to share a story with me about the weather, local sports teams or his family – while he continues to work. The amazing thing is that he does the same thing with all of his customers! He is genuinely interested in people, he loves life, he has fun, and it shows. His enthusiasm is infectious. Customers don't seem to mind standing in line waiting, because they look forward to their turn to interact with Dave. Every time I walk out of that post office I feel energized.

Amazingly, Dave works for an organization employing hundreds of thousands of employees and he stands out amongst all his peers. He could easily choose to come to work each day with a surly attitude, but Dave shows up every day projecting joy and happiness. It is obvious to his customers that he really cares about them and there's no doubt he cares about doing a good job. If you and I will live our lives with enthusiasm, high standards, and a positive attitude like Dave, we will outshine our peers as well!

High Expectations When Facing Adversity

After her stroke Sheryl was forced to endure hours of grueling physical therapy each day for weeks on end. She worked with specialists in speech therapy, learning to enunciate the most common words more clearly, because the right side of her face was paralyzed. She had an arm-and-hand physical therapy specialist, who initiated repetitive exercises hoping to reconnect the brain signals to her right hand and fingers. She also had therapists trying to teach her how to walk again.

A person who is truly driven will overcome their own lack of knowledge and inexperience with their sheer desire to succeed!

While she remained in the hospital, she repeated those exercises painstakingly in an attempt to reprogram her brain. She endured hours and hours of exhausting repetitive drills with a weakened body and injured brain, which caused her to tire easily. Her physical therapists told her she would not be permitted to leave the hospital until she was able to walk from her hospital bed to the bathroom and back under her own power. Hearing that kind of news, many of us would have wallowed in our own self-pity - but not Sheryl. She now had a goal within her own control which motivated her even more. She wanted to walk out of that hospital as soon as she possibly could and she knew she was in control of her own destiny. She was inspired to pursue that goal with all the passion and determination she could muster.

Sheryl participated in her physical therapy twice a day, for weeks on end, with a smile on her face. She had to work laboriously to regain skills which had come naturally to her only days before. She focused on making small improvements each day, which over a period of weeks would lead to a big improvement in her abilities over time. There were days when she made strides forward, and frustrating days when she made no improvement at all, or even regressed. Through it all, she maintained her optimism by focusing on the things she was capable of doing, while not focusing on her limitations.

Imagine, for just a moment, the frustration of being a fully functioning human being one day, and the next day losing the functionality of half your body. Naturally, your mind would become obsessed with comparing your previous capabilities to the things you were unable to do now. You would examine what was once easy to do, to that which is now difficult. Thoughts like, *why did this happen to me?* and w*hat if I am unable to learn to walk again?* would monopolize your thinking. It is at times like this that it is most critical to refocus your brain on positive thoughts; even though the natural tendency is to focus on the negative. Instead of enabling you to succeed, your own negative self-talk and negative thinking can prevent you from reaching your goals.

Amazingly, Sheryl never went down that negative path. Her vision was both positive and clear; her initial goal was to walk out of the hospital under her own power and to do it soon. She dwelled on the positive. She thought about returning to her family and the home she loved. She couldn't wait to sleep in her own bed again, and she dreamed of working in her garden. She fastened her attention on having a positive outcome and that is exactly what happened. It took several weeks of intensive therapy but in the end, Sheryl got up out of her wheelchair, and using a cane, was able to walk gingerly out of the hospital. She accomplished her goal with focus, determination, positivity and high expectations. What she thought about most of the time was learning to walk again, and that is exactly what she did!

It's now been more than ten years since her stroke, and Sheryl is still paralyzed on the right side of her body. She can walk with the aid of a cane, but she has never regained the use of her right hand and fingers. Believe it or not, for the past ten years, she has continued to dedicate herself religiously to going to physical therapy twice a week. That's more than 1000 physical therapy sessions with little if any indication of significant physical improvement; yet, she continues to participate with a positive outlook.

Imagine the commitment, dedication, and passion Sheryl has had to stubbornly continue in the pursuit of a goal with little evidence of improvement in sight... until one day it happened! Sheryl walked into the kitchen, and said she had something exciting to show me. She rested her right hand on the kitchen table and I watched in amazement as she voluntarily moved the little finger on her paralyzed right hand! I had tears in my eyes as she proudly demonstrated her ability to control the movement of an appendage that had been frozen for ten long years. To you, this may not seem like much, but to us, it was a minor miracle!

Sheryl's story of overcoming a catastrophic stroke serves as a great inspirational example of how each of us, with dedication, can overcome our struggles in life. You too have the ability to reach your goals both big and small, but it takes enthusiasm bordering on obsession. It starts with having a goal. *What are you passionate about? Are you willing to persevere when the going gets tough? Can you maintain your commitment even when others tell you it is time to quit? Can you continue to project a positive attitude even when you are faced with obstacles and adversity with no end in sight?*

The Power of Persistence

Sheryl is still able to do most but not all of the things she did before her stroke. She has said she may not be able to work as fast as she once did, but by completing tasks in small pieces over a longer period of time, she is still able to accomplish whatever task she takes on. She believes she can do anything a person with two hands can do, but she knows that it will take her a little longer using just her left hand. As an example, Sheryl loves gardening. She worked for an entire summer planting a fifteen-foot-wide swath of ground cover on a 300-foot-long bank near the road on our farm. She went out and worked rain or shine, for a few hours each day, until she was too tired to continue. The next day, she would be back out there again, sitting on the ground, planting plants, using just one hand. I doubt most able-bodied people with two hands would be able to plant 4500 square feet of ground cover nor would most people be motivated enough to do it. Her example is truly inspirational. When I watch her work, I see passion, persistence, and performance personified!

> In sports, school, business and life, you're almost guaranteed to succeed if you are willing to out-think, out-plan, out-work, and out-execute your peers.

She told me the secret to her success is in the power of taking positive action. She focuses on what she can do, not on what she can't do. She remains positive when many of us would become frustrated or even demoralized. By necessity, Sheryl must break her goals down into smaller pieces, which she then accomplishes systematically, one small piece after another. It's analogous to eating a cake; you can't consume an entire cake in one bite, you eat it one slice at a time. She is extremely disciplined, and she does something each day to move in the direction of completing her goals. Her secret is captured in a positive affirmation she embraces when she takes on big challenges, "*I know yard by yard, everything is hard, but I believe inch by inch, everything's a cinch!*"

Sheryl's example tells us that the way you think, including the attitude you have when you begin, will determine your outcome in the end. She knew her best chance for a successful outcome rested on her ability to remain positive and optimistic for an undetermined amount of time. Under similar circumstances, most of us would have given up. If Sheryl was willing to continue participating in a physical therapy program for ten long years to regain the use of her little finger, imagine what you could accomplish in life if you were willing to invest comparable energy on your goals! Unfortunately, most people lack the kind of passionate commitment demonstrated by Sheryl. You might say she has more passion for achieving her goals in her little finger than most people have in their entire body!

You can *will* yourself to achieve your vision, by having passion, dwelling upon it, putting the effort behind achieving it, and bringing it to fruition. You can accomplish anything you choose to achieve, but it takes total commitment; without it, even your simplest goals can become insurmountable challenges. *Why is it that some people always seem to land on their feet, while others fall down crippled under the weight of life's obstacles? Why do you think one average person experiences great success in life, while another average person doesn't?* In almost all cases, both individuals started out with similar capabilities, talent, and resources. *So, what is the difference?* In my experience, I've found the most prosperous people expect nothing less than the best outcomes. They approach problems as opportunities, they have high expectations, and they accept nothing less than success! They are driven by a can-do attitude as they begin every challenge knowing they will find a way to triumph in the end.

The Story of Your Life

Whether you realize it or not, the story of your life unfolds like the pages in a book. Look back in time and you'll realize the previous chapters of your life have been a series of ups and downs, successes and failures, inspired moments and life shattering letdowns. Regardless of what you've experienced over your lifetime, it is important to remember you can't change your past, though many people waste time trying. Your personal history is what it is. The good news is you do control your present life and you can choose the direction your future takes. You can close the book on your past while setting lofty goals and grandiose plans, of your choosing, for the future. Once you accept the fact that you have complete control over the direction your life takes, you can begin to make the story of your life a dream come true. Live your life each day believing the best is yet to come, because you alone control how this chapter and the next chapters of your life will be written.

The key to unlocking your full potential and writing the story you want for your life starts with having both a vision and a set of defined goals. *Do you wake up each day with a plan or do you simply deal with whatever comes your way? Do you have high expectations for literally everything you do?* Review the following list of statements which focus on *"your personal approach to achieving your goals in life."* Do a self-evaluation by mentally checking off whether the statement accurately describes you always, sometimes, or never.

I am someone who:

	Always	Sometimes	Never
➤ is willing to work hard and make sacrifices to succeed	☐	☐	☐
➤ enjoys solving all kinds of problems	☐	☐	☐
➤ consistently sets my standards higher than others	☐	☐	☐
➤ is willing to take direction from others	☐	☐	☐
➤ enjoys learning new activities and can do it quickly	☐	☐	☐
➤ can influence the views of others	☐	☐	☐
➤ pays attention to detail	☐	☐	☐
➤ can work with others or alone to achieve goals	☐	☐	☐
➤ enthusiastically accepts difficult challenges	☐	☐	☐
➤ consistently makes good decisions	☐	☐	☐
➤ is willing to take managed risks to succeed	☐	☐	☐
➤ asks relevant questions	☐	☐	☐
➤ gets things done on time	☐	☐	☐
➤ talks openly and honestly with other people	☐	☐	☐
➤ listens well when others speak	☐	☐	☐

➢ wants to achieve extraordinary success in life	☐	☐	☐
➢ gets things done the right way the first time	☐	☐	☐
➢ makes commitments and always follows through	☐	☐	☐
➢ accepts and adapts well to change	☐	☐	☐
➢ willingly gives praise and credit to others	☐	☐	☐
➢ shares my knowledge and expertise with others	☐	☐	☐
➢ consistently produces high quality work	☐	☐	☐
➢ builds trust with other people	☐	☐	☐
➢ tries to understand the needs of others	☐	☐	☐
➢ manages my time effectively	☐	☐	☐
➢ easily establishes rapport with others	☐	☐	☐
➢ is effective in taking the lead when necessary	☐	☐	☐
➢ makes certain my efforts always yield results	☐	☐	☐
➢ approaches life with optimism and enthusiasm	☐	☐	☐

The list of statements on this list is actually a *HEATKTE Self-Assessment Questionnaire*. Your answers are an indication of whether or not you have high expectations for everything you do. *Did you find you were comfortable selecting "always" the majority of the time?* If not, the good news is that you can change your approach and make the choice to always embrace those high expectation statements, starting today. This self-assessment can help you decide whether or not you really are willing to make the choice to commit to excellence in everything you do. I recommend you refer back to this self-evaluation periodically as a touchstone to measure your progress along the way on your "*high expectations*" journey!

Saying You'll Do It, and Doing It, Are Two Different Things

The key to accomplishing your goals starts with a vision. *What do you want to do with your life?* Do you have a plan or do you simply go with the flow? I doubt you would travel to a distant destination that you have never visited before without a clear idea of the path you'll take to get there. *Yet in setting sail on your life journey, does your lack of planning indicate you are navigating life's rough waters with a broken compass and no way to steer your rudderless ship?* Without a well thought out plan for your life, you are headed down the path of frustration and mediocrity.

Even people who are doing their best to succeed in life find themselves frustrated from reaching their goals. Millions of hard working people have lost their jobs, are currently under-employed, or are working at a job they just can't stand. If you are one of them, whether you realize it or not, you can choose to take charge of your own life and you can still have it all. You can have a balanced life with a good job, time to spend with your family, financial security and happiness. It may sound too good to be true, but it really is true. That's why if you are willing to blaze your own trail, and persevere when facing obstacles, you can reach whatever goals you set for your life!

> The secret to attaining success in life becomes crystal clear when you discover your life's purpose and you pursue it with passion!

Having goals is one thing. Doing what it takes to turn them into reality is where great plans often unravel. Coming up with good ideas, goals, and a vision are actually the easy part of your life plan; it is the implementation of your life strategies that will prove to be the most difficult. In this book, we will explain how your own high expectations are the key to creating the outcomes you desire in life. As we see it, the personal commitment you make to succeed creates a powerful and unstoppable force that can transform even your most aggressive personal goals into reality! It has worked in our lives and can work in yours too! It also helps that we knew the single greatest secret to success in life.

Life's Greatest Success Secret

Are you interested in learning life's greatest success secret? Here it is: *What you choose to focus the majority of your thoughts, time, energy, and effort upon will virtually guarantee its achievement.* In other words, imagine yourself succeeding by acting as if it is impossible to fail and success will follow. Some refer to this technique as imaging. The idea behind imaging is: what you really focus your mind, body and soul upon ensures, and virtually guarantees, you will achieve that outcome. There is *positive imaging* which leads to good outcomes and there is an equally powerful force called *negative imaging*, which leads down the path to failure. Imaging combines your thoughts, goals, dreams, and aspirations creating an unstoppable force to achieve your imagined outcome. The positive or negative image you imagine and embrace each day becomes a self-fulfilling prophecy.

As an illustration, I'll use my personal experience as an example of imaging. I actually imagined myself becoming an international keynote speaker twenty-five years before I stood on an international stage for the first time in Cologne, Germany. My father encouraged me to become a professional speaker in a discussion we had right after I finished college. From that point onward, I thought about my speaking career almost every day while I gained the necessary prerequisite experience, knowledge, and professional stature. I set about preparing myself by putting a systematic plan in place a quarter of a century before that goal would be realized. The path I followed had plenty of forks forcing me to make decisions, solve problems and adjust my strategy many times along the way. It's still a work in progress, but here's a synopsis of the approach I took.

I started by purchasing a massive, framed, 8' x 10' world map and hung it prominently on a wall in my home so I could imagine myself speaking at exotic international locales around the globe. I also bought a full length mirror, spot lights and a podium which I set up like a stage in my basement. It was there I would practice *"public"* speaking in the privacy of my home. I voraciously read books about strategy, leadership, tactical execution, goal-setting, change management, innovation, business competition, selling, customer service, teamwork, and performance management. I was inspired by the writing of Og Mandino, Zig Ziglar, and Norman Vincent Peale, who filled my mind with positive thoughts and possibilities to build my confidence. I studied great leaders like Michael Eisner, Jack Welch, and Rudy Giuliani, to hone my business leadership skills and knowledge. I shaped my values and reinforced my beliefs by seeking guidance from books written by Joel Osteen, Stephen Covey, and Rick Warren. I read stories of triumph over tragedy by Michael J. Fox, Christopher Reeves, and Randy Pausch, each facing irreversible and debilitating medical conditions. I read books about public speaking, attended speech training seminars, listened to speakers on audio tapes, watched videos of great speakers, and attended live performances to visualize great speakers in action. I spent one-on-one time with successful authors, Peter Garber and Sam Deep, who taught me the secrets behind writing books and articles. I met with storytelling experts, Bill Gove and Jack Boget, who taught me the importance of telling stories to support points made in my speeches and in my books. I invested time and money with professional speaking coaches, Rich Tiller and Somers White, who taught me what it takes to be a successful professional speaker. I found a literary agent, Sam Fleishman, and convinced him to represent me and help me design marketable books that would become the platform upon which my international speaking business would be built. I primed the *"professional speaker"* pump by initially offering my speaking services to meeting planners and conference directors for free, which allowed me to work on my speaking skills in front of live audiences. After all this, I had finally reached a point in my personal and professional development when I knew I had acquired the business maturity, experience, skills, and knowledge required to embark on a professional speaking career. Incredibly, what I thought about and imagined doing for twenty-five years was finally realized when I quit my corporate job and took the risk to become a full-time professional speaker.

Today, I run a successful speaking and writing business. I am the author of six books, and I write articles for publications around the world. I continue to speak at small and large conferences on six continents. As I look back, it took courage for me to walk away from the security provided by my executive job working for a corporation, but I knew in my heart that was what I had to do. With my wife's support and blessing, I pursued the goal I had imagined all those years ago. It took a village of specialists and experts to get me where I am today, and I now know it would not have been possible without their mentorship and guidance. The most important lesson I discovered on my lifelong journey is this: when you work at something that you are passionate about, and that you truly love, it's as if you aren't really working at all!

Continuous improvement is pivotal to your ongoing success; adopt the philosophy that good is never good enough, and everything can be improved upon.

My personal imaging story illustrates the passion and dedication it takes to prepare oneself ahead of time to reach goals in life. I was by no means an overnight success, but due to a lifetime of preparation, I had earned the right to finally be on that stage. The question you must ask yourself is this: *are you willing to dedicate yourself for 5, 10, 20, or even 25 years to achieve your goal if that's what it takes?*

Pursue your Passion

I chose three very different success stories to share with you as examples of people who achieved lofty goals by setting their standards high. Each story is a powerful, yet simple example of how people all around us are making their dreams come true. The stories of Ross, Joan and Jim prove that anybody who has a dream can choose to pursue it, and ultimately achieve it. Like them, I believe each of us has similar hidden talents and aspirations that are just waiting to be fulfilled. Here are their success stories.

When Ross was ten years old, his father took him to the bowling alley for the first time to learn to bowl. His dad was a good bowler, who taught Ross all of the correct bowling techniques. As a result of his father's tutelage, Ross bowled his first 300, perfect game, when he was just sixteen years old. Over the next four years, he rolled 300 seven more times, 299 twice, and 298 once! While still in High School, his bowling average was an amazing 222! The secret to his accomplishments is really no great secret at all. Ross continued to develop his skills by practicing all year round. He bowled several times a week, and perfected his bowling skills as a result. He has passion for the sport, and it shows. He is a great bowler because that is exactly what he has focused his mind on becoming! Now in his twenties, his bowling average has risen to 225, and he has now compiled ten 300 games! He dreamed and focused upon becoming a great bowler, which is precisely what he has become. Ross has already learned what it takes to master a skill with focus and discipline, and you can learn to do it too!

A great example of creating a vision, overcoming adversity, and focusing on reaching a goal is the story of Joan. For a variety of reasons, Joan never had the chance to go to college, to earn her Bachelor's Degree, directly upon graduating from high school. That is not all that unusual as only one percent of the world's population is fortunate enough to earn a college degree. In Joan's case, life happened and she was thrust into the responsibilities of earning a living and raising a family. Amazingly, she never gave up on her dream. Finally, at the age of 54, she enrolled in night classes at a local college, while continuing to work days as a nurse at a hospital. Six years later, at the age of 60, more than forty years after graduating from high school, Joan walked proudly across the stage in her cap and gown having earned her Bachelor of Science Degree in Nursing with Honors. When asked how she did it, she stated, "*I always wanted to go to college and I refused to give up that dream.*" She always knew when the timing was right, she would dedicate herself and make the sacrifices necessary to earn that college degree. She held on to her dream for all those years, and with sheer desire, discipline, and personal sacrifice she accomplished her goal.

Dr. Jim Withers has an unusual vision for his medical career. By day he practices medicine at a hospital, while at night he provides free medical services to the homeless on the streets. His passion for treating the homeless started more than 20 years ago, but he dreamed about helping the homeless from an early age. Many years ago, on a trip to Calcutta, India Dr. Withers met Mother Theresa, who was known for helping the poor while living among them. Meeting her influenced him to establish his "*street medicine*" program called *Operation Safety Net*. He now leads a dedicated team who treat the homeless wherever they live: under bridges, on door steps, and right on the sidewalk. Dr. Withers makes house calls to the homeless and he envisions *street medicine* as a mission of mercy in cities around the world. He figured out a way to pursue his dream as a volunteer providing medical treatment to the homeless at night, while continuing to earn a living working at a traditional hospital during the day.

Whether you are a young adult just starting out like Ross, experienced in living life like Joan, a physician like Dr. Withers, a college student or a business professional you too can find a way to pursue your dreams. When you adopt, *Life's Greatest Success Secret*, you imagine accomplishing a goal and then concentrate your energy on making it happen. If your goal is to become a great golfer, tennis player, or bowler, you must start by thinking and dreaming about becoming great at that sport. Once you've gained the proper focus, you must commit to developing your skills by dedicating yourself to practice. If you desire to become a great nurse or doctor, you must focus on studying to become the best in your field. If your plan is to raise well-adjusted children you must constantly focus on nurturing those young minds. If your goal is to become great in your chosen profession, you must think about refining and achieving that goal morning, noon, and night. Set your sights high and remember most people who fail to reach their goals in life do so not because they set their goals too high, but because they set them too low.

Imagine what might be achieved in our society if parents and educators taught every school age child this lesson. In our school district, there are a number of children, whose parents are from Asia and India, who already embrace this concept. Interestingly, as a percentage of the total student population, these children represent less than ten percent of the total population of students; yet every year, a disproportionate number of Asian and Indian students graduate near the top of their class, based on academic performance. Our school district's high school orchestra perennially has a high representation of students from Indian and Asian descent who are first, second, or third seat based on their musical talent. Here's another amazing example of this phenomenon. In 2013, Arvind Mahankali became the sixth consecutive Indian-American winner, and the 11th in the past 15 years, of the USA Scripps National Spelling Bee.

Are these students somehow predisposed to having a higher IQ or intellect allowing them to perform at a superior level academically? Are they born with academic, musical or memory talents that other students simply don't have? These are obviously very smart young people, but the answer of course is high expectations. Their parents

> Every goal in life is accomplished one step at a time, so answer this question: did you do anything today to move myself one step closer to your goals?

know the value of a great education so they require their children to read, do homework, study hard, and practice every day! Their talents and their accomplishments are a result of hard work. It is not a gift they were born with and it is not a result of luck. Their positive performance is a result of out-thinking and out-working their fellow classmates. The discipline instilled by their parents creates a self-fulfilling prophecy for success. The standards, expectations and attitudes of the parents drive the aptitude of their children. These are powerful examples that prove that what parents and children choose to focus the majority of their thoughts, time, energy, and effort upon will determine and virtually guarantee great academic performance. As a parent, if you have high standards and expectations, your children will too.

Our son, Paul, is profoundly deaf, and he competed in this mainstream, competitive school environment I just described, with the best of the best students. Sheryl, who had experience as a teacher, spent countless hours reading books with Paul, so that his hearing impairment would not be a disadvantage academically. Paul's College SAT scores were so exceptional Sheryl and I have often wondered from whom he inherited his superior intellect. The answer, of course, is not really a mystery at all. Focusing all that time and effort on improving Paul's math, science, and reading skills is the reason why he became excellent academically. His educational brilliance was due to his painstaking, repetitive study, which resulted in the outcome Paul had worked so hard to achieve. What he thought about most of the time was becoming a great student with straight "A's" and superior College SAT's so he could gain acceptance into an Ivy League caliber college - and that's exactly what he achieved!

Paul is intelligent, but unlike a lot of other smart people in this world, he applied himself. I can tell you Paul's secret was a result of hard work combined with the joy he took from learning! As parents, Sheryl and I have high educational standards and high academic expectations, which influenced Paul's outstanding performance.

Any parent can replicate this approach with their children and achieve similar results. *So, why don't all parents adopt this approach?* Perhaps, the time and dedication required is more than most parents can give. Having high expectations alone is not enough; it takes dedication to achieve at the highest level. You can choose to achieve greatness, but it just won't happen without committing to the hard work achieving top performance requires.

Two Gallons in a One Gallon Bucket

If you have children, I know as a parent you must have watched them struggle to write a school paper for one of their classes. *They are often given the assignment at the beginning of the semester, and what do they do?* They wait until the deadline when the paper is finally due to start writing. Typically, they panic, because they don't know what to write or how to write it. *Sound familiar?* I know I watched our teenagers, Heather and Paul, go through this experience a few times.

I have a theory I developed based on my observations of the procrastination of children, who wait until the last minute to write those papers. I call it my *two gallons in a one gallon bucket theory.* Here is how the theory works. If a child has a school paper to write, that paper represents a one gallon bucket, into which they must pour at least one gallon of knowledge. Often children want to take the easy way out when it comes to doing the research for their school papers, and they end up with only a half gallon of knowledge to pour into that one gallon paper. It is no wonder writing that school paper is so frustratingly difficult! Those children, who get the *"A's"* on their papers consistently, have a secret. They do a great deal of reading and research for their school papers before they start writing. When it comes time to actually write the paper, they start out with much more than a gallon of knowledge to pour into that one gallon paper. Writing is easy when they have a great deal of knowledge about the subject.

This same theory goes far beyond the confines of a school paper. It is equally applicable to procrastinating adults, who may be taking the easy way out in the pursuit of their goals. *Have you invested the time to gain all the knowledge it takes to perfect your craft? Have you dedicated the time it takes to become an expert at what you do?* If you want to achieve anything significant in life, you must pay the price by investing the time to increase your knowledge. Interestingly, once you gain the one or two gallons of knowledge to pour into your one gallon career bucket, you'll find everything you try to do is easier. You'll gain confidence as you increase your consistency of attaining success, because you have done your homework! Show me someone, whom you perceive as an expert, and I'll bet their expertise is a result of having *two or more gallons of knowledge* to pour into their one *gallon bucket of expertise*. It's a choice they made to be an expert by mastering a body of knowledge via study, hard work, and application. They transformed themselves into becoming what others now perceive as an expert.

After my first book was published, I was a bit puzzled when my international speaking business took off. I had been speaking professionally for years, and my personal knowledge and expertise wasn't any different from the day before my book was published to the day after. Something had indeed changed; it was the perceptions of others towards me. By acquiring several gallons of knowledge in my field and then pouring it into that one gallon book, the perceptions of others changed, and in their minds, I was now perceived as a bona fide expert in my field. By developing your expertise, the same thing can happen to you!

Creating a Slight Competitive Edge

Look at the peers with whom you grew up and you'll find most of them ended up a member of the herd of average people. Each of them had an equal opportunity to achieve at the highest levels yet very few actually did. *Why is that? Were the high achievers somehow predestined to greatness?* I think the answer comes down to two all important factors: setting aggressive goals coupled with disciplined execution. I explained it this way to my daughter and son. Most high achievers are average

> If you are going to compete and you hope to win, always go into the competition expecting to win, and the outcome can become a self-fulfilling prophecy.

people who set and achieved lofty goals simply by applying themselves with extraordinary discipline. They take what they have learned in life and do the best they can with their God-given talents. Their competitive advantage in life is a clear vision, indomitable passion, and methodical application. The highest achievers make the sacrifices the average members of the herd won't make, can't make, or are unwilling to make.

The following thought-provoking passage illustrates the importance of not only having knowledge; but also applying that knowledge to achieve at the highest level. I excerpted and adapted this passage from the *"Two Young Men"* letter written by Martin Conroy.

Two young men graduated from the same college and they were very much alike. Both had been better than average students, both were personable, and both - as young college graduates - were filled with ambitious dreams for the future. Recently, these men returned to their college for their 25th reunion. They were still very much alike. Both were happily married, both had three children, and both as it turned out, had gone to work for the same Midwestern manufacturing company after graduation, and were still working there. But there was a big difference. One of the men was manager of a small department of that company. The other was its president.

Have you ever wondered, as I have, what makes this kind of difference in people's lives? It isn't always raw intelligence, or talent, or dedication. It isn't that one person wants success and the other doesn't. The difference lies in what each person knows and how he or she makes use of that knowledge. These two young men graduated from college together and together got started in the business world; so what made their lives in business so different? It was knowledge, and, more importantly, the application of that knowledge, creating a slight edge that made the difference.

By applying your knowledge and expertise, you too can gain that slight edge that will make you the best in your profession. It's true! The difference between being good at what you do versus outstanding at what you do really isn't that much. It is a simple choice you make to differentiate yourself by always maintaining a slight edge compared to similarly qualified people around you. It's about consistently applying yourself, and focusing your energy, to out-think, out-work and out-execute your peers. If you'll give just 5% or 10% or more effort to everything you do, you will create that edge, and you will become outstanding compared to your peers in whatever you choose to do! As an example, start by simply starting work an hour earlier and working an hour longer every day, and you will begin to outperform all of your peers. Most self-made millionaires would agree that working longer hours is one of the most important prerequisites to achieving success.

If you're in sales, imagine how your performance would improve if you would just make one or two more sales calls each day, That's more than 200 additional sales calls per year! The difference between good and outstanding in sales is just 5% or 10% more effort each and every day. It is a choice you make or don't make to achieve greatness. If you desire to be a top percentile performer in whatever you choose to do, just consistently work longer and harder than all of your peers. That's the secret of the greatest golfers, tennis players, baseball, and football stars. They aren't

100% better than the great athletes around them; it's more likely they are just a small percentage better. They show up early for practice and stay late. They've learned the secret to creating a slight competitive edge and it is those extra hours of practice that really make a difference.

What about you? If you were put on trial today, accused of being outstanding in your field, would there be enough evidence to convict you? Do you get to work early and stay late? Do you make the sacrifices necessary by always giving that extra effort, to gain the knowledge, experience, and expertise to become the best you can be? It's not just about showing up. It's about applying yourself by gaining the knowledge and experience required to master your craft. When you truly are perceived as outstanding in your field, you've created substantial distance between yourself and the rest of the competition. At that point, the sky's the limit on how far you can go and the best news of all is that no one can stop you. By creating even the slightest competitive edge, you put yourself out ahead of the herd and in control of your own destiny.

Opportunity comes disguised as hard work and problems . . . so if you are a problem solver willing to work hard, your opportunities are endless.

In business, it is quite common for organizations to strive for excellence. Companies have high expectations as they culturally integrate values like continuous learning, continuous improvement, and embracing change. *Why do high performing companies worry about getting even better?* It's because they know their past success doesn't guarantee they will succeed in the future. The business world is highly competitive when it comes to attracting customers, retaining customers, and growing market share. Company executives have a dual focus. They must run their day to day operations, while at the same time steering a course into the future. The challenge they face is making sure they have the right products and services in place to match the changing marketplace. They understand their company's past accomplishments do not guarantee that they'll continue to be profitable in the future. The best companies are constantly reinventing themselves to ensure relevance today, as well as tomorrow. They identify what they are doing right, and more importantly, they identify what they need to improve upon. Never satisfied, the great leaders challenge the status quo in hopes of finding the slightest competitive edge. Having high expectations in the world of business is not a choice as much as it is a necessity for survival!

Turning Vision into Reality

I had a rare opportunity to travel to Memphis, Tennessee to tour the FedEx airport hub at night. I arrived at the airport at 9:00 at night and toured the FedEx hub until after 4:00 in the morning. Like clockwork, the planes, loaded with packages from around the world, arrive and leave the FedEx hub with precision every day. By 4:00 in the morning, all of the planes are re-loaded with packages for the return trip back to wherever they originated. Amazingly, Fred Smith, the founder and visionary behind FedEx, was spurned by others in the package delivery industry when he first proposed his overnight package delivery concept.

People didn't believe Fred Smith's ideas would succeed because they were revolutionary and had never been tried before. One of the critical components of his service strategy was designed to challenge existing package delivery practices. We all can remember the days when the U.S. Postal Service was known for its ineptness delivering mail to our homes in a timely manner. It is still referred to as *"snail mail"*. The FedEx design was meant to change the way packages were to be delivered around the world, forever. As a result, the U.S. Postal Service was forced to become more efficient at delivering its mail and packages by studying and adopting many of FedEx's groundbreaking logistics and delivery strategies.

One of the most important secrets to Fred Smith's strategy was the high expectations he set for timely package delivery by his drivers. You see, Fred Smith had two rules for serving his customers: *the first, never promise more than you can deliver, and the second, always deliver on what you promise.* So when FedEx first started delivering packages overnight, he crafted those rules into an aggressive delivery standard, which all of his package delivery people had to meet. In FedEx's early advertising, they made an ironclad commitment, *"We will absolutely, positively get that overnight package to you by 10:00 in the morning."* Fred's rules became a standard and a performance expectation for his drivers in the form of a *"delivery affirmation statement"*, which was then reinforced each day by FedEx's customers. Fred Smith's high standards became FedEx's high service standards, causing his customers to raise their expectations. Fred set the bar high and it was now up to the thousands of FedEx employees to deliver upon that promise.

Fred Smith's high expectations had single-handedly transformed an entire industry by raising delivery standards and simultaneously raising consumer expectations of all package delivery companies. His new and better way of delivering packages created a sustainable, competitive advantage FedEx has enjoyed for decades. In the process, the FedEx brand has become synonymous with fast package delivery in the same way Kleenex has become synonymous with tissue. Fred Smith achieved his dreams by setting what most viewed as unrealistic goals, standards and promises, backing it all up with a no excuse delivery guarantee for his customers, and expecting his FedEx delivery team to fulfill those promises. Fred Smith had a vision and he turned it into reality.

What's your purpose on this planet?

You too have the ability to turn your passion into reality. To do it, you have to do some soul searching, and you must ask yourself some tough questions. *What goal in your life are you not currently pursuing that you may someday regret not having pursued? Could you accomplish something great if you were willing to take the risk to achieve your goal? What are you really good at that could possibly become your life's work?* As you ponder the answers to these questions here is an illustration of that point from the wisdom of Mark Twain:

A man died and met Saint Peter at the gates of heaven. Recognizing the Saint's knowledge and wisdom, he wanted to ask him a question. "Saint Peter", he said. "I have been interested in military history for many years, tell me, who was the greatest general of all times." Peter quickly responded, "That is a simple question, it is that man right over there." The man looked where Peter was pointing and answered, "You must be mistaken, I knew that man on earth and he was just a common laborer." "That's right", Peter remarked, "but he would have been the greatest General of all time, if he had been a General."

Have you identified what you were put on this earth to do? Do you have a great idea, dream, vision, or passion that you are not currently pursuing? You should listen to that sometimes irritating, inner voice that may be questioning the path you are currently on. *Do you sometimes feel the same frustration that laborer must have felt who could have been a great General?* Only you know the answer to these questions. Remember this: you've only got one life to live and one chance to live it. Each of us was placed on this earth with an equal opportunity to make a difference in the world, so discover your unique purpose and pursue it! If you pursue what you are passionate about in life, when you reach the end, you'll have no regrets. Unfortunately, too many of us will close our eyes for the last time without ever having realized our full potential.

You can achieve extraordinary results in life if you are willing to blaze your own trails, challenge the status quo, and take calculated risks.

Hold on to Your Dreams

A couple of years after Sheryl suffered her stroke; it appeared she would never be able to drive her car on the road again. One day, I took her out for a test drive in a large empty parking lot. As hard as she tried, she struggled mightily. She desperately wanted to drive her car, but her reflexes weren't what they used to be. She found driving with just one hand not only difficult, but dangerous too.

One day, our teenage daughter, Heather, asked me *why I didn't just sell Mom's car since she will never be able to drive it again.* I looked Heather in the eye and said, *"I will never sell your mother's car. It will remain in the garage forever, even if the tires dry rot off the wheels. That car represents a symbol of freedom and hope for your mom. As long as that car is there, she knows there is a chance that she just might drive again one day."*

Many people who face frustrating barriers to achieving their personal goals are unable to remain positive. They lose their fighting spirit, but not Sheryl. Ever since her stroke, she has focused on what she can do, not on what she can't do. She exercises as aggressively as she can and her persistence has paid off. She learned to walk again. She can't walk far, but she can get around our two-story house. She has even learned how to climb up the stairs, walking forwards, while walking down the stairs backwards! When we travel, she takes her wheelchair because she tires quickly if she must walk long distances. Her tenacity is truly inspirational, and her indomitable spirit is something for others to admire and emulate. She has high expectations, and she does whatever it takes within her own ability, to reach her goals! She may not be able to drive that car, but she continues to have passion bordering on obsession for accomplishing the important things in life. *Do you?*

HEATKTE
(Pronounced: Het-**Ka**-Tee)
Key to Success #2

High Expectations Are The Key To Everything

HEATKTE Keys to Success

KEY #1: VISION & PURPOSE

KEY #2: PLAN & STRATEGIZE

KEY #3: EFFORT & EXECUTION

KEY#4: AFFIRM & BELIEVE

KEY#5: ACHIEVE & SOAR

KEY#6: PERSEVERE & OVERCOME

HEATKTE Key to Success #2

■ PLAN & STRATEGIZE ■

I must develop a personal plan of action because
if I don't, others will plan my future for me!

When our children were young, the neighborhood parents would take turns driving each other's kids to soccer practice. When I say *parents,* I really mean *mothers.* So, like all the other soccer moms, I took my turn as *Mr. Mom* driving our daughter, Heather, and her teammates to practice in our minivan. I would usually have five or six of the neighborhood kids onboard for the trip to the soccer field. Being a motivational speaker, I relished the idea of having a captive audience, even if it was five or six children in my van, for the 10 minute drive!

14 Transformational,
Two-Letter Words:

*If It Is To Be,
It Is Up To Me,
To Go Do It!*

As I drove down the road one day I asked the kids, *"Do you want to know one of the great secrets to doing well in life?"* They actually responded *"yes"*, they were interested in knowing. I said, *"The secret is a 14-word phrase, and each of the words has only two letters."* Now, it was a bit of a mystery so they really seemed excited about knowing the secret. Using my best, motivational voice, I said, *"If It Is To Be, It Is Up To Me, To Go Do It!"* They were fascinated! Picture Mr. Mom, driving down the highway each time I drove those kids to soccer practice saying *"repeat after me, If It Is To Be, It Is Up To Me, To Go Do It."* Years later, every time I have seen one of those youngsters, who are now young adults, I have asked them to repeat those 14, two-letter words. Every single one of them still remembers and repeats them back to me with enthusiasm!

To take control of your own destiny, you too must embrace the simple philosophy, *If It Is To Be, It Is Up To Me, To Go Do It! What are you waiting for?* No one is going to hand you the keys to a better future; you must take charge of your own destiny! If you find yourself waiting for someone else to take you to the answer for what you need to do with your life, you're going to be frustrated forever. Reassert control of your own life by living each day as an empowered individual who goes out and makes things happen. So, repeat after me: *If It Is To Be, It Is Up To Me, To Go Do It!* Embrace the simple message contained in these 14, two letter words, and you're on right path.

So the question is how do you get started? It all begins with the choices you make. When you stop worrying about what everybody else thinks, and start doing what you know you really want to do, everything changes. You become more focused, more committed, more passionate, and more willing to do whatever it takes to overcome the obstacles ahead. *So I ask again, what are you waiting for?* The days of your life are limited so don't waste your valuable time trying to live up to someone else's expectations for your life. Your future is in your hands so choose the path you'll take wisely; your destiny awaits!

Unfortunately, many people never get the chance to do what they really want to do because life happens. They are forced to lower their expectations due to unfortunate circumstances like the loss of a job, and with it, the loss of security having a regular income provides. If you are suffering, because you are unemployed, underemployed, or unhappy in your work, you are part of a growing segment of our society. But it doesn't always have to be that way. There are other alternatives that still allow you to take charge of your life. If you are willing to step back and develop a personal plan of action, and consider alternatives, and possibly even a change of direction, you may just find your personal key to happiness. When you figure out what your passion really is and you actually begin pursuing it, you put yourself on your unique path to a successful and joyful life. We live in a world where you can do whatever you wish to do, and you can be whatever you want to be. There are examples of people achieving their dreams all around you, so make the choice to be one of them.

When I spoke at a conference in Caracas, I had dinner one evening with a group of frustrated business people. They told me as entrepreneurs, they were unable to reach their full potential, because the socialist government in Venezuela created many insurmountable financial obstacles for businesses trying to grow their sales and profits. They longed for the chance to practice free-market capitalism like the entrepreneurs in other countries in North, Central, and South America. On the return flight home to the USA, I thought about what they had told me, and I must admit, it saddened me. I found an inspirational quotation that captures the spirit of those Venezuelan, wannabe free market capitalists, which I have since quoted in my speeches around the world. It seems the perfect way to compliment this discussion about controlling your own destiny. These words, written by Dean Alfange, which I've paraphrased, are intended to bolster the spirit of anyone who is frustrated trying to achieve their goals in life.

I do not choose to be a common man (or woman). It is my right to be uncommon - if I can. I seek opportunity - not security. I do not wish to be a kept citizen, humbled and dulled by having the state look after me. I want to take the calculated risk; to dream and to build, to fail and to succeed; I refuse to barter incentive for a dole. I prefer the challenges of life to a guaranteed existence; the thrill of fulfillment to the stale realm of Utopia. I will not trade my freedom for charity, nor my dignity for a handout. I will never cower before any master nor bend to any threat. It is my heritage to stand strong, proud and unafraid; to think and act for myself, to enjoy the benefit of my creations and to face the world boldly and say: this, with God's help, I have done. All of this is what it means to take control of my own destiny to achieve my dreams!

It is important to take control of your own destiny, because if you don't do it someone else will be quite happy to control your future

Having enthusiasm, passion, and commitment is the right recipe for not only meeting, but also for exceeding your goals!

for you! Unlike those wannabe free market capitalists in Venezuela, you have a free choice to reach your full potential. If your current profession, job or role in life isn't fulfilling, you can make the decision to change directions. You have more control than you may think. If you feel otherwise, it may be because you have given the responsibility for controlling your future to someone else. If you are one of the lucky ones who is happy with the direction of your life, your job, and your chosen career: congratulations, many people would love to be in that same position.

Having worked in the corporate world as a Human Resources Executive, I've talked to hundreds of people about their jobs, careers, goals and aspirations. Based on my experience, I can tell you the organization you work for will not relinquish control of planning your future career opportunities or your future compensation as long as you work for them. Early in my career, I still remember being told by the executive I worked for that the company would manage my career on my behalf. Plain and simply put, the organization I worked for expected to manage and control my future and my career for the benefit of the enterprise. That didn't sit well with me. It was that moment when I decided to quietly take back control of the direction and timing of my own career.

Engagement – How Loyal Are You?

A business acquaintance of mine, Jim, is a long term employee at the headquarters of one of the largest companies in America. After 30 years of employment, he has finally reached a junior level executive position. He has job security, steady pay, benefits, and a good financial package to look forward to when he retires. *Sounds like a dream come true, doesn't it?* Most of us would envy what Jim has accomplished, and we'd love to be in his shoes, but that's not how Jim feels. As far as he is concerned, his career progression has stalled and he is frustrated at having to do the same work year after year. Worst of all, he feels he is not growing professionally. He feels guilty that he didn't pursue goals of his choosing because he gave his company complete control of his career.

Although Jim believes he has more to offer in life, he is stuck in a career rut from which he will never escape. He believes he can't afford to strike out on his own and do what he believes he was put on this earth to do. He has a home mortgage, two children in college, bills to pay and he is worried about having financial security for his retirement years. He told me he would like to quit his secure job to pursue his real passion but he can't because the risk is too high and he is afraid he'll go broke. Many of us share the same founded and unfounded fears as Jim. Unfortunately, it is those fears that prevent us from doing what we really want to do in life.

When he considers changing direction, Jim only sees the problems, instead of the opportunities for someone with his credentials. Franklin Roosevelt aptly described Jim's situation when he said, *"Men (and women) are not prisoners of fate but only prisoners of their own minds."* Jim visualizes the people around him facing financial ruin. In his mind, he pictures his neighbors who have been laid off, friends who are unemployed, people who are underemployed, jobs going overseas, and companies going out of business. He feels lucky to have a steady paycheck in this economy. He's taken the position that his personal career frustration will end, and his personal happiness will begin, when he retires. He rationalizes that is when he'll pursue his real dreams.

It takes tremendous courage to stay focused on your dreams when others tell you that you're destined to fail.

Jim is not alone. A recent Forbes Magazine article reported, *"Only one in five workers is "fully engaged" in his or her work."* That statistic translates into millions of workers who are frustrated with their careers: employees, managers, and executives who hold jobs for which they no longer have a 100% commitment. Most like Jim would like to make a change, but due to fear, they feel helplessly stuck right where they are. They have the skill but not the will. They go through the motions but their hearts aren't in it. I describe the commitment level of people like Jim, which according to Forbes Magazine is 80% of the workforce, as *"disengaged"*.

Unfortunately, Jim continues to work at his corporate job day in and day out. He is suffering and his company's bottom-line suffers too. As long as he collects a paycheck, he'll show up for work every day looking the part as he continues to go through the motions. Unfortunately, his heart isn't in it and his commitment to the work hasn't been there for years. His passion is long gone and his spirit has been defeated. To paraphrase Henry David Thoreau, *Jim's work life, like that of so many others, has become one of quiet desperation.*

Why is it that so many of us can relate to Jim's situation? That's because there are three distinct types of commitment levels people have out in today's work world: 1. Employees who are *fully engaged*, 2. Employees who are *partially engaged*, and 3. Employees who are *totally disengaged*. *As you read the following "commitment level" descriptions, try to determine which category you, and your fellow employees, fall into.*

COMMITMENT LEVEL I:
Fully Engaged – "Both Feet In"

In the old days, there were people who actually remained engaged and committed to their work throughout their careers. My father is a good example. He was one of those who started his career just after World War

II and worked for the same company for 30 years. In those days, if you had a good job, you stayed with it until you retired. In some cases, generations of the same family worked for the same company from "*cradle to grave*". Those employees, who received a pension upon retirement, were willing to forgo greener pastures for the lifelong security their companies provided. Those employees, like my father, were loyal to their companies so they felt engaged, happy, and fully committed to their work. Companies and their executives were also loyal to their employees fully expecting them to retire from their jobs. Like many people from his generation, my father was fully engaged and excited about his work and the security it provided for his family. He had what I would characterize as a *both feet in* level of commitment. Those who were fully engaged rarely thought about changing jobs; in those days, people grew where they were planted.

In case you haven't already figured it out on your own, the days of fully engaged employees with the guarantee of lifetime employment is a thing of the past. The loyalty once experienced by employees from their employers during my father's time is now long gone. The new reality for today's workers is strikingly different. A large portion of the older population, who in days gone by would now be comfortably retired, are now forced to work at minimum wage jobs to supplement their paltry savings. Today, most of us are responsible for financing our own retirement years and for paying for our own retiree medical insurance. Many people are already experiencing a lower quality of life in their golden years than that of members of previous generations. We must all face the fact that it's up to each of us to selfishly look out for our own short and long term interests!

COMMITMENT LEVEL II:
Partially engaged – "One Foot In and One Foot Out"

Today, whether we like it or not, most of us are facing a new and harsh reality. Employer loyalty has become an oxymoron. Modern day employees are experiencing layoffs, cutbacks, companies going out of business, and some companies even moving their entire operations along with our jobs overseas. I heard a telling statistic that half of those who are currently employed are dissatisfied with their jobs and are actively looking for a better job! That means those who are lucky enough to have a job are frustrated and disgruntled, but they are smart enough to stay put until they find something better. Employees are dissatisfied with their paychecks, lack of opportunity for personal growth, limited opportunities for career advancement, lack of recognition from their supervisors, and feeling trapped in jobs they don't like. They show up for work each day, but clearly they aren't fully engaged in their work, nor are they committed to the company they work for. Biding their time, they do just enough good work to get by, prepared to quit as soon as that next better career opportunity comes along. *Does that scenario sound familiar?*

The best strategy embraced by many workers today is to remain partially engaged, continuing to work for their current employer, while simultaneously searching for what they *perceive to be a better job*, at what they *perceive to be a better company*. I call this new level of job commitment, straddling the job loyalty line with a psychological commitment level characterized by having *one foot in and one foot out. How can organizations expect to prosper with so many unhappy employees and loyalty levels at an all time low?*

COMMITMENT LEVEL III:
Totally Disengaged – "Both Feet Out"

I can relate to Jim's story, and people like him, because my personal career story is very similar. I was a corporate guy, who had worked for twenty-five years in several large companies. I had job security because I was very good at my profession. I received an excellent salary and outstanding benefits that made my family's life comfortable and our future secure. *What did I have to complain about?* Nothing really, but my job commitment was gone. Psychologically, I would characterize my commitment level as having *both feet out*. Towards the end of my corporate career, I showed up for work every day, and I continued to do a good job, but my heart clearly wasn't in it. I got to the point where I was

> Each of us has a calling in life, and if you're lucky enough to find yours you are on the path to personal success and happiness.

totally disengaged, as if in my mind I had already quit, even though my body was still showing up for work every day. I knew I had been put on this earth for another more important purpose and it was time for me to go out and realize that dream. So, after a quarter of a century working in the corporate world, I quit the rat race to begin pursuing my life's passion. Of course, it was risky being an entrepreneur, and at times, I second-guessed my decision. There were even times when I checked out the employment ads, but in the end, I stayed the course. Now, I call the shots, I am responsible for paying my bills, and I alone decide how I will spend my time. I made the tough decisions that were right for me and as I look back, I have no regrets.

You Don't Choose Your Passions in Life, Your Passions Choose You!

Let me ask you a question, what level of commitment do you have for what you do? Are you totally committed with both feet in, do you straddle the commitment line with one foot in and one foot out or do you clearly have both feet out like Jim? Are you unhappy doing what you are doing, knowing in your heart you'd rather be doing something else? If you lack passion for what you're doing now, give serious consideration to what you would really prefer to do with your life. Each and every one of us has a unique gift or talent and your passion in life is likely to be connected to it in some way.

Whether you believe it is in your DNA or divinely implanted, the fact is: *You don't choose your passions in life, as much as your passions somehow magically choose you!* For some, it is like a fire burning inside their belly; for others, a quiet voice inside their brain. Mine was a combination of raging fire and nagging voices driving me to pursue my dreams. Today, I love what I do and it shows! I wouldn't want to do anything else and I am completely committed with both feet in!

How do you recapture passion for your job, your marriage, your family, or your education? Though you may not think so, you are not at the mercy of the system where you work, your supervisor, a pay scale, the educational system, or a bad family life. Your time is limited so don't waste it living someone else's life, because you have alternatives. You can choose to change your circumstances and it starts with figuring out what you would do. Maybe you are currently doing something you love and you are already pursuing your dreams. I hope you are but here is a question to test that theory: *If asked on your deathbed whether you had any regrets about the way you spent your time on earth, would you talk about what you would have, should have, or could have done, or would you enthusiastically respond: I have no regrets. I pursued my dreams!*

It starts with a vision, now what's your plan?

So, how do you get started? It starts with a vision or overriding goal that clearly defines what you expect to accomplish. Then, you must challenge yourself to become a continuous learner with a constant focus on improving your knowledge, skills, ability and overall expertise. It helps to have values like honesty, integrity, and fairness along with a strong work ethic. Your future goal attainment will be determined by how well you solve the myriad of problems you will face and how well you convert good strategies into action. Obviously, having a vision is not enough. Until you develop a plan of action, nothing will happen. Unfortunately for many, developing a plan and setting goals is a painful process. But once you do, you will begin to realize there really is a cause and effect relationship between setting clearly defined goals and attaining them. This realization is the starting point for taking control of your future. When you set your own goals in life, you call the shots, and you alone are responsible for the good and the bad results.

> When you set goals for your life, don't be afraid to dream big, because surprisingly, the tendency for many people is to set their goals too low!

If you find yourself struggling to define your goals, it should be no surprise why you are frustrated. The simple fact is: you can't accomplish goals that you can't clearly articulate! Many good intending people adopt a *"ready, shoot, aim"* approach to goal achievement. They err on the side of action, by creating a flurry of activities without first identifying their final destination. For this reason the single most important contributor to goal achievement is starting with a well, defined goal. The second key ingredient is the development of a strategy. Finally, the ultimate ingredient is the implementation and execution of the strategy. Once you decide what you are going to achieve, you need to commit your goal to paper with a well thought out plan of action.

For something to actually become your goal, it must be personally important to you. You can choose to set goals in various areas of your life including: financial, health, personal relationships, self-development, spiritual, your job and your career. You can set short term and long term goals. *What is it that you would you like to accomplish? What areas of your life would you like to improve?* Once you can answer these questions, you can then begin to create a clearly defined and focused goal statement. From there, you can begin to get more specific in the development of your personal plan of action. Write your goal in the form of an affirmation. Here is an example I used earlier in my career: *I will gain the knowledge, experience, and training necessary, to become a Vice President of Human Resources for a Fortune 500 company before I am 40 years old.* Remember to set your goals high by remembering: high expectations are the key to everything!

A Simple Five Step Goal-Setting Process

The following five steps are intentionally written in a simplistic way to make the whole goal-setting process less intimidating. These steps are the foundation upon which your success will be built. Goal-setting is the strategic part of your success model, which is defining the target and how you will get there. The hard part is the implementation of the tactics required to achieve your goals. Remember: ninety percent of any good strategy is the successful execution of it!

Goal Step #1: Clearly Define Your Goal

Be clear, what do you want to accomplish? A vague or poorly defined goal has little chance of ever succeeding. As an example, a college student might have this goal: I want to graduate from college. That may be true, but a clearer goal for that same student would state: I will graduate from college in four years, with a 3.0 or higher GPA, with a Bachelors of Science Degree in Marketing, preparing me to get hired by a Consumer Packaged Goods Company. When your goal is clearly defined, you know it will be focused and you'll have a clear idea what you are trying to achieve. Ask yourself this question:

- *Is your goal both easy to understand and specific?*

Goal Step #2: Make It Quantifiable

Think about what you want to achieve and then come up with a way to assess and measure your progress along the way. A clearly defined measurement gives you quantifiable feedback of where you stand in relation to your goal! Goals that are measured have a greater tendency to actually get accomplished. Ask yourself this question:

- *Is my goal quantifiable / measurable?*

Goal Step #3: Set It High

Is the goal you set within your capability to attain? You should always set your goals just out of reach so you must always stretch to achieve them. Goals that are too easy or overly difficult may not motivate you to action. Ask yourself this question:

- *Do I have the resources and motivation necessary to attain my goal?*

Goal Step #4: Do You Have the Resources?

Is the goal you've set realistic given your knowledge, experience, and time available to pursue it? To give your best concentrated effort, you must be able to devote adequate time and your focused attention to achieving your goal. Ask yourself these questions:

- *Given the other time commitments I already have in my life, is the goal I have set realistic?*
- *Do you have the knowledge, skills, education and ability required?*

Goal Step #5: Develop a Timetable

Have you set a completion date or deadline for completing your goal?

One of the biggest inhibitors to goal attainment is procrastination. When you add a time element, you hold yourself accountable. Operate with integrity when you set your goals by doing what you say you're going to do, when you say you are going to do it! Ask yourself this question:

- *Have I held myself accountable by making my goal time-bound?*

Goal, Plan, Execute, Track & Achieve

During the time I was writing this book, I set a goal to lose weight based on my doctor's recommendation. I decided to put a **Five Step Plan** in place to help me accomplish this goal. My vision was **Step 1** of my plan: *I wanted to lose 50 pounds in four months by modifying my diet and increasing my exercise.* Once I had a clearly articulated goal, I could now develop the rest of my plan around it. For **Step 2,** I developed a specific highly modified diet, and an aggressive exercise program which would guarantee attainment of my

> The measure of your success in life is the obstacles you have overcome.

weight loss goal. To satisfy **Step 3**, I needed to make certain I had the resources I needed so I bought a treadmill, which I set up in my basement, allowing me to exercise conveniently at home. **Step 4,** I decided to measure my progress, by logging my weight and exercise activity on a chart, which tracked my daily progress towards my goal. Finally, at **Step 5,** I set up a timetable to exercise every other day for four months to reach my goal. *Was my goal realistic and was my plan achievable?* You'll find out in the chapter discussing *HEATKTE Key to Success #4* in this book, where I provide a detailed description of the outcome of my "diet and exercise five step plan.

You now know a simple five step process to assist you in accomplishing your goals in life. Unfortunately, many people try to operate without a plan and they wonder why they fail to consistently hit their ill-defined targets.

Those who set up a plan find they have more control of achieving their targeted outcomes. It is important to find some quiet time each week to step back from your busy life to evaluate your plan and adjust your strategy. When you do, your confidence will improve as you experience the satisfaction of knowing you are moving your life proactively in the right direction! Once you achieve a goal, take time to celebrate your success, and immediately set a new goal that makes you stretch even higher!

Plant a Stake in the Ground

My father told me a great story about the time he and my grandfather planted a small sapling in their backyard. To assure the tree grew straight and tall, they cut a branch from another tree to use as a stake to provide support for the sapling as it grew. For some unknown reason, the sapling they planted died, while the branch they used as a stake sprouted leaves and grew! Think about that; the tree died, and the stake grew! From this story, I learned a valuable lesson about planning which I have used many times to my own advantage.

The planning of my first trip to Australia paralleled my father's story. I was hired to speak in Sydney at a conference that was scheduled for July that year. Since I had six months to prepare, I contacted other companies in cities across Australia to announce I was coming. I created a flurry of activity about my pending trip, and as a result, I contracted two additional speaking engagements in Brisbane and Melbourne, also in July. What happened next amazed me. The speaking engagement in Sydney, which was the original reason for my trip, was cancelled. Metaphorically, the Sydney conference was like that tree my dad had planted that had died; the Brisbane and Melbourne speaking engagements were like the stakes that grew. By putting a stake in the ground, you might say I had snatched success from the jaws of failure! You can do it too. Plant your own stake in the ground by developing your own back-up plan, just in case your original plan either changes or fails.

HEATKTE
(Pronounced: Het-**Ka**-Tee)
Key to Success #3

High Expectations Are The Key To Everything

HEATKTE Keys to Success

KEY #1: VISION & PURPOSE

KEY #2: PLAN & STRATEGIZE

KEY #3: EFFORT & EXECUTION

KEY#4: AFFIRM & BELIEVE

KEY#5: ACHIEVE & SOAR

KEY#6: PERSEVERE & OVERCOME

HEATKTE Key to Success #3

■ EFFORT & EXECUTION ■

> I intend to achieve extraordinary rewards in life, so I am prepared to face my fears to achieve my goals.

Have you ever thought about reinventing yourself by taking your life in an entirely new direction? Most of us have had at least passing thoughts about what we'd really like to do with our lives if we were guaranteed to succeed. Few people actually take the risk because of the fear of failure. Human beings have many other deeply rooted fears including: heights, spiders, tight spaces, darkness, and germs. There are also other fears we bow to every day that may prevent us from reaching our goals in life. Those fears include: financial concerns, relationship issues, family trauma, health concerns, marital problems, job loss, change, and failure. Regardless of any fears you experience, I hope you realize you do have the power and capability within you to conquer your fears and move your life in a new direction!

Be a Willing Protégé:
Explain it to me, and I will understand…
Teach me, and I'll know how…
Give me a chance, and I'll prove I can do it!

The very thought of changing directions and taking risks in life fills many people with one of the most paralyzing fears of all - the fear of the unknown. Of course, if you suddenly find yourself experiencing a midlife crisis because you are unemployed or underemployed, fear can also be a powerful motivator of positive change in your life. When you have nothing to lose and no other choice, you are more open to reinventing yourself by necessity. Circumstances force you to move in an entirely new, different, and possibly even more exciting direction. But still most of us think, *why take the risk?* Given the choice most people would prefer the security of a solid, uninspiring job, to the alternative of the unemployment line; an unhappy relationship to no relationship at all. You may settle for less than you really deserve because you figure, *what choice do I have?*

Some have chosen to accept their lot in life because of their upbringing or the expectations set for them by others. The vast majority of people follow the herd because that's all they've ever known and besides they figure that's what everyone else does. Here is a parable many of us can relate to because, like the elephants, many of us were conditioned to accept less than our full potential by others starting at an early age.

As I was passing the elephants, I suddenly stopped, confused by the fact that these huge creatures were being held by only a small rope tied to their front leg. No chains, no cages. It was obvious that the elephants could, at anytime, break away from the ropes that bound them but for some reason, they did not.

I saw a trainer near by and asked why these beautiful, magnificent animals just stood there and made no attempt to get away. Well, he said, when they are very young and much smaller, we use the same size rope to tie them and, at that age, it's enough to hold them. As they grow up, they are conditioned to believe they cannot break away. They believe the rope can still hold them, so they never try to break free. I was amazed. These animals could at any time break free from their bonds but because they believed they couldn't, they were stuck right where they were.

Like the elephants, many of us go through life hanging on to a belief that we cannot do something, simply because we failed at it once before, and we stop trying? Why is it that we give others permission to directly or indirectly take control of our lives?

Get Out of Your Comfort Zone

One of the reasons you may feel uncomfortable *reinventing yourself*, going in a new direction, and takings risks is because of your own self-imposed comfort zone. Think back to when you were a youngster, a time when most of us, without much thought, were willing to try risky and even scary new activities. As adults, we developed commonsense and with that the desire to remain in the safety and security of our comfort zone, because it's a place where we know exactly what to expect. By being risk averse and maintaining the status quo, we can avoid the possibility of the negative consequences associated with risk-taking. If you use that approach to your life, you'll simply maintain things just the way they are, and if you're lucky, you'll live a pretty average life. The need to have a safe and secure routine, at the expense of the potential rewards offered by trying something new and exciting, may doom you to a dull and monotonous existence.

Breaking free of your comfort zone always requires that you make some kind of change, and change can be downright scary. Whether you perceive a change to be positive or negative makes little difference; change has always been uncomfortable for human beings. Given a choice, most people would choose to maintain things the way they are because they dislike the disruption and uncertainty associated with changes in routine. By simply changing your routine and trying something new, you may trigger positive changes in your life. Face it, you can't continue doing things the exact same way you have always done while expecting a new and exciting breakthrough result. Said another way, the same effort and activity will always yield the same old unsatisfying result. By changing your approach, challenging your fears, and striking out in a new and unfamiliar direction, you will force yourself to break free of your comfort zone.

A great example of breaking free of my personal comfort zone occurred on a recent business trip I took to Australia. I knew the famous Sydney Harbor Bridge offered a unique view of the Sydney Opera House that can only be experienced by climbing to the top of the bridge. I had wanted to climb the bridge on each of my previous trips to Australia but I avoided it because of my fear of heights. I made excuses that I didn't have the three hours necessary to complete the climb due to a tight schedule. On this particular trip, I had the time and I was committed to confront my fear of heights. Without a great deal of forethought, I walked from my hotel and purchased a ticket for the next bridge climb scheduled to start a few minutes later. Before I knew it, I was hiking to the top of the Sydney Harbor Bridge, four hundred feet above the water. Interestingly, I never had thoughts of backing out once I had made the commitment by purchasing that ticket. I also didn't experience high anxiety before, during, or after the climb. I rationalized that more than 2 million others had already made the climb before me and all had arrived back safely on the ground. By voluntarily forcing myself to confront my fear, I discovered I could choose to overcome what I thought was a debilitating fear of heights. My perception of my fear of high places, before I started the climb, was far worse than the reality I actually experienced during the climb. Interestingly, in the end I discovered I didn't really have a *"fear of heights"* as much as I had a *"fear of falling"*. Once I was convinced there was no way to fall off the bridge, my initial fear was transformed into exhilaration and the thrill of enjoyment.

> Most strategies that fail do so not because the strategy itself was flawed, but because it was so poorly executed.

Trust Your Gut Instincts

Taking precautions when making difficult decisions in life is constructive, but living in a state of constant polarizing fear of making a decision is downright debilitating. It may seem counterintuitive but the less time you spend analyzing the pros and cons, the good points and bad, when making day to day decisions, the more likely you are to make the right decision for your life. When it comes to the big "whether you should or shouldn't" life decisions, like home buying, quitting a job, making a career change, starting a company, or getting married, a risk averse mindset can cause you to over-evaluate minute details while wasting valuable time procrastinating unnecessarily. In the end, when you succumb to the paralysis of analysis you are likely to make worse decisions than you would have made, had you simply trusted your gut feelings and been decisive. Not surprisingly, the fear of making a wrong decision can prevent you from making any decision at all! So trust your gut instincts, get off the fence, and make the tough decisions. Accept the fact that there are no guarantees in life and sometimes you will make mistakes. By trusting your intuition, you are bound to make the right decisions the majority of the time.

When I graduated from college, I was determined to get my career started, but unfortunately, I couldn't find a quality career opportunity in the area where I lived. I found a low paying job, which I took just to pay my bills. I searched for 6 months after graduation to no avail. Initially, I had hoped to stay close to home, but because of the poor economy and high unemployment in our area, there was no reason for an employer to hire someone like me who lacked real-world experience. Though I preferred to stay close to home, circumstances forced me to take the risk of moving far away. That risk paid off quickly when I found a good-paying job in Houston, Texas. Finally, I was on my way to establishing my career. At the time, I was reluctant and a bit fearful of moving to Texas, but I really had no choice. Surprisingly, once I gained experience, I ended up moving back to where I grew up, and this time, because of my experience, I had no problem finding a great job.

When our daughter Heather graduated from college, she too ended up moving far from home to establish her career. By necessity, she took a big risk by moving far away, but she was rewarded with a great career opportunity. I recommended this strategy to others who were struggling to get their careers started, and not one of them was willing to pick up and move somewhere else to pursue opportunities. When you have few options, it is imperative to do something proactive to give good things a chance to happen. Heather found a great job because she was willing to get out of her comfort zone and do what so many others are either unable or unwilling to do. *Are you at a crossroads in your life? Are you willing to step out of your comfort zone and move in a new unfamiliar direction?* It worked for Heather and it could work for you too! To paraphrase the words of the poet, Robert Frost, two roads diverged and she took the one less traveled, and that has made all the difference.

It takes courage, commitment, and confidence to break out of your comfort zone, but that doesn't mean you should be reckless. There is a big difference between reckless decision-making and taking managed risks. You should always think through what you want to do and weigh the various consequences of your decisions and actions. Only when you are willing to accept the risks and understand the possible consequences should you consider moving forward.

Adapt, Survive & Thrive

My ancestors are from Sweden and my surname , *Bergdahl,* means *"mountain valley"* in Swedish. It is an interesting coincidence that the Bergdahl family now lives in a mountain valley on a small farm in Pennsylvania. Remarkably, Sheryl and I live just a short distance from where we grew up and originally met. A beautiful stream runs across our property and our pond attracts a wide variety of wild animals including: white tailed deer, wild turkeys, ducks, and geese. Due to hunting restrictions in our area, most of the wild animals thrive.

Surprisingly, I never see pheasants on or around our farm which I remember seeing when I was a child growing up in this area. For this reason, Sheryl and I decided to purchase and release several pheasants on our farm to help repopulate these native birds. We contacted a local farmer who raises pheasants, which he sells to restaurants. The farmer agreed to sell us as many pheasants as we wanted but, knowing where we lived, he cautioned us that the pheasants would not survive. He reminded us that the area where we lived had been overrun by urban sprawl and the kind of natural habitat necessary for the survival of pheasants no longer existed in our locale. He said the natural predators of the pheasants would quickly hunt down all of the birds we released, foiling our plan. Skeptical, I questioned the farmer about why the wild turkeys that had also been reintroduced in our area were thriving. We didn't understand why the pheasants couldn't adapt and survive as well.

To strike out in a new and unfamiliar direction, you must be willing to get out of your comfort zone, take risks and embrace change!

The farmer asked me a revealing question that unlocked the secret to the survival of turkeys versus pheasants in the wild. He asked, *"Do you know where turkeys and pheasants sleep at night?"* That question surprised us and the answer surprises most people. The farmer explained that turkeys can fly so they spend the night sleeping high up in trees. Even though pheasants can also fly, they choose to spend the night sleeping directly on the ground. Over the years, as their habitat was eliminated, due to home construction and habitat destruction, the pheasants became easy prey for night prowling predators. That's exactly why pheasants are now extinct in the area where we live and why turkeys continue to thrive. Those turkeys are smart. They've stopped focusing on basic survival every night by choosing the security of spending the night in the highest branches. Unfortunately, those pheasants are content on expending less energy by staying close to the ground where survival is most difficult, if not impossible.

This survival story of the pheasants and turkeys is analogous to the success metaphor of people choosing to expend the energy to gather "*low versus high hanging fruit*". Given the choice, most people stay on the ground, stretching only as necessary, avoiding risk of climbing higher, as they compete with the masses on the ground to pick the limited fruit within easiest reach. Of course, the greatest rewards are to be found by the few individuals who are willing to expend the energy by taking the risk to climb up into the branches to pick the unlimited supply of high hanging fruit.

Which of these best describes you? Are you a risk-averse ground dweller, or are you someone who is willing to take your chances climbing to new heights? Is your objective simply to survive or is it to really thrive? Is your plan for your life to hunker down and hope for the best, or is your life strategy to spread your wings and soar to explore new and exciting possibilities? These are important questions for you to ponder, because the bounty you gather in life is a product of how much energy you are willing to spend and how much risk you are willing to take.

The story of "*pheasants versus turkeys*" and "*low versus high hanging fruit*" reminds me of my Psychology 101 class in college which taught Maslow's "*hierarchy of needs*". That psychological theory states that people must satisfy lower level safety, security and survival needs before they have a chance of reaching their full potential. Maslow refers to reaching life's pinnacle as achieving a state of "*self-actualization*" which is the achievement of one's full potential through creativity, independence, spontaneity, and a grasp of the real world. Unfortunately for many people, progress in life towards achieving significant personal goals is often disrupted by the need to focus on basic survival needs thus eliminating the chance to reach that all important state of self-actualization. Of the more than seven billion people in the world, only 1% of them actually ever reach this level! If you are lucky enough to be one of the few self-actualized individuals, you are a lot like those turkeys who are thriving because they made the choice to stretch, reach, and soar to the top. Most people, however, are struggling to meet their basic security needs, so they are like those ground dwelling pheasants fighting for life's scraps in a struggle each day simply to survive.

Accepting Failure is Not an Option

Look around you and you'll see several distinct kinds of people. There are those who never made it because they tried and failed and then decided to never try again. They muddle through life dissatisfied with their lot in life, and with what they have accomplished, but they won't do anything about it. There are people who live paycheck to paycheck, struggling to just make ends meet, never discovering a way to truly flourish. Finally, there are those, who are experiencing various degrees of achievement despite past challenges and even failures. The difference for them is that they have remained driven to achieve great success as they solve routine problems and overcome major obstacles.

When you choose to achieve great success in life, in actuality, you have chosen the path of most resistance! Think of someone you know who you think has achieved at a high level. It is almost certain that individual has faced challenges, overcome adversity, and even faced down failure! The most accomplished people aren't lucky, more gifted, or more visionary than others, but they are more focused. Their success isn't a result of predestination, kismet, destiny, luck or fate. They have a plan, they are willing to take action, and they are willing to work hard to turn their goals into reality. They believe in inventing their own future, knowing they can't wait for others to hand them the keys to prosperity. Each day, they go out and create their own opportunities, and they aren't afraid to take calculated risks. Top performers are life-long, continuous learners, who often have a network of mentors, upon whom they rely. Sometimes they make mistakes and sometimes they fail along the way, but they always get back up and continue to fight.

Everyone Faces Failure

My first attempt to become a published author actually failed miserably. I have no excuses. It was my fault. I had written a book that no publisher was interested in publishing, because no reader would be interested in reading it! I poured my heart and soul into writing that first book, and when it wasn't published, I felt like I had been punched in the stomach. Imagine writing 300 pages, more than 100,000 words, and wasting six months of your life - that's exactly what I had done. The wounded feelings and humiliation of that first failed book writing attempt lingered within me for a very long time.

After failing, like I did the first time, here is the question I now faced: *would I be crazy enough to consider trying to write a second book?* I had concerns about my own ability. Those doubts were the biggest hurdle I had to overcome in order to start writing again. You see, writing a book takes hours and hours of sitting at a blank computer screen, alone with your thoughts. If you don't believe in yourself, and you're not fully committed to what you're writing, it just doesn't work very well. When you have doubts and fears about your own ability, it's like a batter stepping up to the plate trying to hit with two strikes against him. That's exactly how I felt.

Once again, it was Sheryl who provided the inspiration I needed by encouraging me to write that second book, and amazingly, she challenged

Most of our fears are worsened by our own imaginations. When you face your fears, you open yourself up to a whole new world of exciting possibilities.

me to do it from her hospital bed! She said that if she could dedicate herself to learning to walk again; with my knowledge and experience, I could surely sit down and write another book. It was just the *kick in the pants* I needed at that point in my life to get me moving again! As I now reflect back on my first book writing fiasco, I must admit that I learned some valuable lessons that prepared me for doing a better job the second time around. So, I picked up my broken ego, dusted it off, and decided to try again. This time I found mentors who had experience writing successful books. They were instrumental in guiding me, and with their help, I wrote diligently for six months crafting another 300-page manuscript. The outcome on my second book was quite different then my first effort. This book was bought by a publisher immediately upon completion and has now been published in countries all over the world in ten different languages!

This success story is a great example of how having high expectations and a good attitude can overcome self-doubt and even past failures. There are actually many positive lessons to be learned from mistakes and failings, which can become the solid foundation upon which future success is built. That's exactly what happened to me!

Each of us will fail from time to time, but the important thing is how you respond. Many famous people were forced to overcome adversity, negativity, or failure in their lives, before they were able to achieve great success. Here are several examples of well-known people who dealt with failure before they ultimately triumphed.

- *Henry Ford failed five times before he succeeded.*

- *Thomas Edison made hundreds of unsuccessful attempts before he finally invented the light bulb.*

- *The BEATLES were rejected by Decca Records because producers didn't like their music.*

- *Albert Einstein was late learning to speak/read, so his parents thought he was mentally slow.*

- *Michael Jordan was cut from his high school basketball team.*

- *Bill Gates was a college dropout.*

- *Walt Disney was fired by a newspaper editor because he had no imagination.*

- *Colonel Sander's original chicken recipe was rejected by hundreds of restaurants.*

- *James Dyson built dozens of vacuum cleaner prototypes before he found the one that worked.*

- *Abraham Lincoln was defeated in several elections when he ran for public office.*

Isn't it interesting that many well-known, highly successful people went through the same kind of frustration and failure faced by you and me? The lesson to be learned from them is they didn't give up, and in the end, through their efforts, our society and the world have been changed for the better. They proved that setbacks are temporary and can actually lead to even greater success in the future. Here is a tribute to people like them (written by Steve Jobs) who go out and make a difference in the world while risking the possibility of failure.

"Here's to the crazy ones, the misfits, the rebels, the troublemakers, the round pegs in the square holes... the ones who see things differently -- they're not fond of rules... You can quote them, disagree with them, glorify or vilify them, but the only thing you can't do is ignore them because they change things... they push the human race forward, and while some may see them as the crazy ones, we see genius, because the ones who are crazy enough to think that they can change the world, are the ones who do."

Remember these examples the next time you are struggling. If some of the most successful people the world has ever known overcame adversity to achieve the fame for which they are now known, you and I can do it. By being willing to stay the course to overcome life's obstacles, you may end up being one of the crazy ones who really makes a difference in this world too!

Build It and They Will Come

I was very fortunate to get the chance to personally work one-on-one with one of those world-changing visionaries, Sam Walton, the founder of Walmart. Early on in his career, Sam was forced to face his fear of failure and overcome financial obstacles to achieve the great success for which he is known today. By the end of his life, Sam had amassed a personal fortune of more than one hundred billion dollars! He was by no means an overnight success. He toiled and struggled to bring his retailing dream to fruition for decades. The behind the scenes story that most don't know about Sam Walton is that he almost failed. You see, few people believed his idea of opening large retail stores in small towns would succeed. For Sam Walton, the end had to feel near when local banks refused to lend him money. Those bankers thought his business model was illogical and could not possibly work. Then, his product suppliers refused to sell him merchandise unless he paid for their goods in cash, upon delivery. They too concluded he would fail. Even many of the local citizens, who liked the products he offered in his store, believed a small town could never be able to support such a huge store. Sam Walton must have felt like the whole world was lining up against him, with most betting his inevitable failure was just a matter of time. Under those difficult

When others criticize your ideas, what they are really telling you is not that YOU can't do it, but that they know THEY can't do it!

circumstances, Sam Walton had to have tremendous courage; he had to remain steadfast when all of those around him questioned his judgment. Sam seemingly had no one to turn to for assistance or guidance, so he relied on his faith in God and the support of his family. As it turns out, all of those early critics were wrong. His company not only survived, it thrived, and it was Sam Walton who ended up having the last laugh when his company became the world's largest!

Purposeless People Dislike People With Purpose

Sam Walton's story is inspirational for a reason. We've all experienced similar negative feedback when we tell others about our aspirations. Our goals may not be as big as Fred Smith's or Sam Walton's, but we all have things we'd love to accomplish if we could find the courage. The problem is the naysayers. There are plenty of people quite willing to tell you that your ideas will not work and that you will fail. *Does that sound familiar?* Those bad intending know-it-alls, who are always quite willing to predict your future demise. They love to throw cold water on your good ideas and tell you what you can and can't accomplish. It's as if they are a crystal ball reader, which has given them the unique ability to accurately predict your future. But, I suggest you take a look at their lives and ask these questions: *how is their purported future vision working for them? Are they some kind of great role model or have they achieved success in their own life that warrants following their advice?* Often, you'll find they are quite the opposite. What they are actually saying to you is that they can't do it, which doesn't mean you can't do it! Certainly, there are good intending people who give you valid feedback that you should definitely consider. But don't listen to the naysayers, the good intenders, the know-it-alls, or the ne'er-do-wells, because most of the time, they have absolutely no basis for their opinions. Their goal is to steal your courage, and along with it, your dreams. When

I hear the naysayers, in my own life, trying to tell me what I can and can't do, I reject their unsolicited feedback. I ask them to get out of my way, so I can prove I can do it. Don't allow someone else who may have given up on achieving their dreams to talk you out of achieving yours!

In the future, when you are confronted with unwanted criticism, shift your focus to these inspirational words of encouragement by Theodore *"Teddy"* Roosevelt titled, The Critic:

It's not the critic who counts; not the man or woman who points out how the strong man stumbles or where the doer of deeds could have done them better. The credit belongs to the man or woman who is actually in the arena, whose face is marred by dust and sweat and blood, who strives valiantly, who errs and comes up short again and again, because there is no effort without error or shortcoming, but it is the man or woman who actually strives to do the deeds who knows the great enthusiasms, the great devotions, who spends himself or herself in a worthy cause; who, at the best, knows, in the end, the triumph of high achievement, and who, at the worst, if they fail, at least they fail while daring greatly, so that their place will never be with those cold and timid souls who know neither victory nor defeat.

Unfortunately the same kind of undeserved negativity and unwarranted criticism experienced by successful CEO's like Fred Smith and Sam Walton is happening all around you as well. That's why, when you have a good idea you need to really believe in yourself, especially when it's apparent no one else does. Accomplishing difficult goals is often complicated by the barrage of negativity from people closest to you. If you think everyone actually wants you to prosper, think again. *Do you realize that some people, including peers, friends, and even your extended family members, do not want you to differentiate yourself from them by becoming more accomplished than they are?* Your good fortune in some strange way may even be perceived as some kind of threat to them. Don't be surprised if you get the feeling they want you to do well, but not too well! It happens to people all over the world and it could be happening to you. Here's why.

Tall Poppy Syndrome

On the first trip I made to Australia, I learned one of the reasons why even famous people experience undeserved negativity from the people around them. The Australians call it *tall poppy syndrome* (TPS). TPS is a social phenomenon whereby the highest achieving citizens are resented, attacked, cut down, or criticized simply because their achievements are perceived to elevate them above other average people. The symbolism behind TPS is that by *chopping down the tallest poppies in the field, no individual poppy is allowed to stand out above all the others.* In this unfair and hostile environment, imagine how many people never even try to reach their full potential, settling for average levels of success or even mediocrity, out of fear of being labeled and treated like they are a tall poppy. What a ridiculous waste of human potential. Tall poppy syndrome is a universally recognized phenomenon occurring in different variations in countries and cultures around the world. TPS is the desire to cut down to size any person, who is considered to be too successful, supposedly for their own good. It is the nasty politics of envy. Tall poppy syndrome occurs as a direct result of jealousy, and the intention by those who use it is simply to unfairly punish those who are viewed as amazingly talented or extraordinarily famous or wealthy.

> One of the most satisfying experiences you will have in life is accomplishing one of your goals that others told you couldn't be done.

As a result of TPS, there are Australian citizens who have refused to accept the offer of Knighthood by the Queen of England, because of the fear of negative consequences associated with being perceived as a tall poppy. Paul Hogan, who starred in the Crocodile Dundee movies, and

Steve Irwin, the Crocodile Hunter, were both mercilessly criticized by their fellow citizens because of their global notoriety! Nicole Kidman, the actress, is loved by fans around the world but many of her fellow Australian citizens verbally attack her just because they are enraged by, and jealous of, her fame.

Variations of tall poppy syndrome happen to achievers around the world. When Christina Aguilera was 18-years old, she was already an international singing sensation. She decided to attend her high school senior prom, where she was shunned by her jealous peers. Fellow students refused to even dance to Christina's hit songs when they were played at the prom! Julia Roberts was similarly mistreated when she attended her high school reunion. Not surprisingly, tall poppy syndrome isn't limited to just the rich and famous. It can also afflict anyone who experiences a high degree of wealth, fame, or success in life that differentiates them from their former peers!

Like Crabs in a Bucket a.k.a Misery Loves Company

The *crab in the bucket concept (a form of TPS)* is drawn from the real life example of the behavior of a bucket full of live crabs. As the story goes, if you catch one crab and put it in a bucket, you must put a lid on the bucket because that crab will do everything within its power to try to crawl out of that bucket or it will die trying. If you put two or more crabs in a bucket, you don't need to put a lid on the bucket. When one of the individual crabs tries to crawl up and out of the bucket, the other crabs will grab it from below and pull it back in before it can reach the top.

Just like the illustration of the crabs in a bucket, the same thing happens to people like you when you strive to outshine your peers. As an example, in some of our most disadvantaged communities, those who are striving to build a better life are actually criticized, and belittled by their own neighbors. The same kind of thing is happening around you too: in businesses, government, volunteer work, hospitals, schools, student groups, labor unions, churches, and anywhere else you are around a group of your peers. It doesn't make sense, but believe it or not, some of the people closest to you may find your accomplishments contemptible and like those crabs in the bucket they want to pull you down to their level.

Gore Vidal, the American writer, put it this way when he said, *"Every time a friend succeeds I die a little."* Strong emotional feelings of negativity like these are prompted by simple jealousy, and possibly even rage, at life's unfairness. The jealousy is a result of knowing that one's peer, who began life as an equal, is now pulling ahead in life. The rage stems from the fact that they know in their heart they will never be equals again. Secretly some of your peers, friends and family members may feel exactly the same way as Vidal Gore, when confronted with your success! This is why you must keep your guard up while maintaining a degree of skepticism when evaluating the recommendations made to you by your friends, family, and peers.

A good example of this happened when I told my peers, at the company where I worked, that I was leaving to go to work for Sam Walton. My peers and my supervisor advised me to reconsider. Some of those naysayers went so far as to tell me I was crazy to even consider leaving. At that moment, the pressure to stay was withering and it would have been easy to accept their advice. The hard thing to do was to trust my own instincts even though I had no idea what the future would hold. As it turned out, my decision to leave had been the correct decision. As I look back, who I am today is a direct result of making many of these same types of difficult, personal, and life altering decisions.

Stop worrying about pleasing everybody else and start worrying about your own happiness. Accept the fact that any decision you make will in all likelihood be second guessed by those around you. Do it anyway. You have one life to live, and it's your right to live it the way you choose. Identify your dream, and selfishly pursue it. Take the advice of Mark Twain who said, *"Keep away from people who try to belittle your ambitions. Small people always do that, but the really great ones make you feel that you too can become great."*

To achieve personal excellence, start your own self-development program by becoming a lifelong continuous learner!

According to research conducted by Professor Michelle Duguid, from Olin Business School, there are specific factors that keep women from helping one another get ahead in business, which are driven by paranoia. Duguid conluded that after years of being outnumbered in the business world, some female executives actually fear other highly qualified female peers and associates who might appear to be more qualified and competent then they are. Additionally, women who have made it to the top are afraid of appearing as though they're looking out for one another. Even worse, a workplace bullying study showed that female bullies targeted other women in the workplace about 70% of the time. This phenomenon is analogous to tall poppy syndrome adding to the difficulty women experience trying to get ahead in the corporate world.

So let me ask you a question: are you guilty of trying to sabotage the success of others? If so, it's a tremendous waste of your time and energy! You'd be far better off spending that same time focused on developing your own skills, building your own network or actually helping others succeed. Badmouthing others is not only destructive to them but to you as well. You would be far better served building others up, helping them, and even praising their accomplishments. When you learn to be truly happy with the good fortune of others, rather than envious and resentful, good things will begin to happen for you as well! Benjamin Franklin Fairless, the former CEO of U.S. Steel, put it this way, *"You cannot strengthen one by weakening another; and you cannot add to the stature of a dwarf by cutting off the leg of a giant."* The strategy of pulling other people down to build yourself up is a loser's strategy that ultimately ends in mediocrity all the way around.

You Were Meant to Shine

When you are confronted by unwarranted criticism from your peers, friends, family members, or any naysayer, I want you to remember you still have the right and responsibility to strive to be the absolute best you can possibly be. Don't ever allow those small minded people around you, to shake your confidence, and divert your attention away from striving for greatness. The following inspirational verse called, *Our Deepest Fear,* written by Marianne Williamson, describes how each of us must shed our fears and gives each of us permission to pursue greatness.

Our deepest fear is not that we are inadequate. Our deepest fear is that we are powerful beyond measure. It is our light, not our darkness that most frightens us. We ask ourselves, who am I to be brilliant, gorgeous, talented, fabulous? Actually, who are you not to be? You are a child of God. Your playing small does not serve the world. There's nothing enlightened about shrinking so that other people won't feel insecure around you. We are all meant to shine, as children do. We were born to make manifest the glory of God that is within us. It's not just in some of us; it's in everyone. And as we let our own light shine, we unconsciously give other people permission to do the same. As we're liberated from our own fear, our presence automatically liberates others.

Marianne Williamson's inspirational words illustrate that many of us actually fear our own potential success, but why? Maybe it is because we feel like we are undeserving, or it could be because others will take offense if we tell them about our good fortune. Stop feeling guilty for achieving success in life, and stop hiding your successes from the world. You have the God-given right to become the best that you can be, so you have permission to shine!

Confronting Your Fears

My father taught me a valuable lesson around the time I had started my first job. He was an excellent speaker who often spoke at business meetings where he worked; he also enjoyed speaking at Lions Club and Rotary Club Meetings. He told me that one of life's greatest fears, shared by the majority of people, is the fear of speaking in front of groups. It is actually a recognized phobia called *glossophobia,* which is defined as the *fear of public speaking.* The symptoms of *public speaking phobia* include intense anxiety, physical distress, nausea, and panic, which may cause the individual to avoid attending events where they might be asked to say a few words in front of a group. Experts say one of the keys to overcoming this phobia is building self-confidence by mastering the topic. The unfortunate consequence of having a fear of public speaking is that executives tend to select future leaders based on how well they present their ideas in group meetings.

My dad was a mechanical engineer who worked on complex projects at a large corporation as a member of a team of engineers. When it came time to present the project results to the corporate executives for financial approval, the project team always nominated my dad to make the presentation. He told me the other engineers were as smart as he was when it came to engineering, but he was the only one who had no fear of making the presentation of the team's multi-million dollar engineering projects to the company's executives. So, every time a project was presented for approval, he was the guy the team nominated to present it to the top executives. You can guess who got promoted. My father emphatically told me that the single most important skill for people to master is the ability to present their ideas one-on-one or in front of a group. In business and life, he said, there is no single skill that will take you further than being a skilful thought leader, who is able to comfortably present thoughts, opinions, and ideas.

As you set sail on your life journey, is your lack of planning an indication that you are navigating life's rough waters with a broken compass and no way to steer your rudderless ship?

Due to the importance of this lesson, we shared my father's story with our children when they were still in elementary school. We did not want Heather and Paul to fear public speaking, so from an early age, we told them that speaking in front of groups was something they should look forward to doing. The fear surrounding public speaking is often reinforced and taught to children by their own parents. If asked, most people would admit they are scared to death to give a speech. The unnatural fear that they have of public speaking is shared with their children, creating a negative, self-fulfilling prophecy. The fear of speaking is a myth that has been perpetuated by fearful parents for generations. In actuality, there is nothing more natural than presenting your ideas to others. Because of our influence, both of our children are comfortable speaking in front of groups. They have no fear of it, and they actually look forward to it! We created a positive, self-fulfilling prophecy that will give them a competitive advantage, regardless of the path they choose in life. You can become a skilled and fearless public speaker and if you are a parent your children can too!

Many years ago, I attended a 14 week public speaking class to develop the right techniques for public speaking. An important benefit of the training is that I learned how to overcome the stomach butterflies we all experience when we are about to present our ideas in front of a group. I can still remember that first public speaking class like it was yesterday. The teacher asked each of us to prepare and present a simple two-minute speech to our classmates, introducing ourselves and describing our background. There were twenty of us in the class, which is a large enough audience to make most speakers a little bit nervous and even downright uncomfortable.

One after another, we rose to deliver our two minute introductory speeches and all of us did it without a hitch. But then it was Mary's turn and something happened that I will never forget. Mary walked up to the front of the room and turned to face the class. She stood there for what seemed like an eternity without uttering a single word. Her mouth was open, but no words were coming out! I remember how uneasy it made me feel, watching her suffer. The teacher refused to intervene, intentionally, allowing us to fully experience Mary's anguish. Minutes went by as we watched Mary's body trembling from fear, and tears streaming down her cheeks. Finally the teacher stepped in to end our collective misery. Strangely, as we all watched Mary suffer, we felt like we were suffering too. The teacher told us that what we had just witnessed was a severe case of stage fright. Incredibly, he said, when people are asked about their greatest fear, they will consistently name *"fear of public speaking"* or *"fear of getting up in front of an audience,"* as their number one fear, right up there ahead of spiders, snakes, and even death!

Some of the most well-known performing artists have admitted to suffering from some degree of stage fright, including Donny Osmond, Kim Basinger, Laurence Olivier, and Barbra Streisand. As an example, Barbra Streisand began suffering paralyzing stage fright when she forgot the words to several songs during a concert in New York's Central Park. From then on, Streisand was worried that she might embarrass herself again if she performed in public, so she totally avoided live performances for 27 years. In recent years, Streisand started performing in public again by starting with a smaller warm up show, then a national tour, and finally performing live in front of a large television audience. The gradual accumulation of positive responses to her performances led to a change in Streisand's thinking, and she has now performed in public many times since.

Reaching your goals in life is ten percent vision and ninety percent going out and making it happen!

As I watched Mary, I remember thinking to myself I will never see her again, because surely she will drop out of the class after having experienced nothing less than public humiliation. I was wrong, Mary did not give up. She came back and attended every class for the next 13 weeks. The transformation in Mary was nothing short of astounding. By the time we got to the last class, Mary had become a skilled, articulate speaker, who actually enjoyed public speaking. Of course, she won the class award for being the most improved speaker!

In watching Mary go through what she went through, I learned a powerful lesson about making a commitment to overcoming fear. If the same thing that happened to Mary had happened to most of us, we would have walked away defeated. I asked Mary why she continued attending after her disastrous start to the class. She said she suffered from a paralyzing fear of public speaking her entire life, and that fear was preventing her from achieving some of her goals in life. She said she had signed up for that public speaking class voluntarily, knowing she would be forced to confront her greatest fear. Mary wanted to conquer her fear of public speaking to improve her life, and that's exactly what she did. In all my life, Mary's courage stands out as one of the finest examples of confronting fear that I have ever personally experienced. Mary's lesson has three components, from which we all can learn: confront your fears, don't give up even when you feel defeated, and believe in your ability to overcome any obstacle.

What fears stand in your way as you ponder strategies for tackling your life's challenges? If Mary was willing to suffer public humiliation to confront her greatest fear, you must take on your fears as well, knowing you too can succeed! So the question is: w*hy not get started now?*

HEATKTE
(Pronounced: Het-**Ka**-Tee)
Key to Success #4

High Expectations Are The Key To Everything

HEATKTE Keys to Success

KEY #1: VISION & PURPOSE

KEY #2: PLAN & STRATEGIZE

KEY #3: EFFORT & EXECUTION

KEY#4: AFFIRM & BELIEVE

KEY#5: ACHIEVE & SOAR

KEY#6: PERSEVERE & OVERCOME

HEATKTE Key to Success #4

AFFIRM & BELIEVE

> I will do something each day to move in the direction of my goals.

I remember sitting in Carnegie Music Hall, a proud father, watching my daughter Heather play a viola solo as a member of a symphony orchestra. As I sat there, I recalled all the years of private lessons she had endured, and the personal sacrifices she had made to become a talented musician. She was committed to her dreams and the result was the opportunity to perform before a large audience in a great concert hall. As I watched and listened to her viola solo that day, I realized her great accomplishment in music was a direct result of her long term vision, self-sacrifice, discipline, and dedication. Luck wasn't a contributing factor; it was her own hard work

Approach the adversity you face in life as a cause to be overcome, and use it as a source of personal inspiration.

and commitment to her goals that provided her with the opportunity to achieve musically at the highest level. Her many successes in life instilled confidence and as a result she graduated from college with both a Bachelor's of Science Degree and an MBA. Still driven to achieve more, she spent another year taking pre-med courses which prepared her to pass the Medical College Admission Test. She was then accepted into medical school.

That same kind of passionate determination exhibited by Heather is required to achieve most worthwhile endeavors in life. You can have all the raw talent in the world, but failing to put forth your best effort is a common reason for coming up short. This parable, called *The House You Build*, provides a great illustration of that point:

An elderly carpenter was ready to retire. He told his employer of his plans to leave the house-building business and live a more leisurely life. He would miss the paycheck, but he needed to retire. His boss was sorry to see his good worker go and asked if he could build just one more house as a favor. The carpenter said he would, but in time, it was easy to see that his heart was not in his work. He resorted to shoddy workmanship and used inferior materials. It was an unfortunate way to end a dedicated career. When the carpenter finished his work, the employer came to inspect the house. He handed the front-door key to the carpenter exclaiming, "This is your house, it is my gift to you!" The carpenter was shocked! What a shame; if he had only known he was building his own house, he would have done it all so differently.

So it is with us. We build our lives, a day at a time, often putting less than our best efforts into the building. Then with a shock, we realize we have to live in the house we have built. If we could do it over we'd do it much differently, wouldn't we? But we cannot go back. You are the carpenter; each day, you hammer a nail, place a board, or erect a wall.

You might say all of our lives are ongoing do-it-yourself projects. The quality of our work each day builds the *"house"* we will inhabit tomorrow. Heather's house is built on a solid foundation because she worked hard and she practiced diligently to be the best. As in Heather's example, always build your house with pride to the best of your ability!

Change Your Habits

It may sound harsh to hear, but the truth is that many people lack the discipline required to accomplish challenging goals. Even objectives that are well within their ability become insurmountable tasks. *Have you ever known someone who tried to lose weight or quit smoking?* At the beginning, they talk proactively and convincingly about changing their bad habits. Though they start with the best of intentions, most fail after a short period of time. *What happened to that initial burst of enthusiasm and excitement for achieving their goal? Why did they lose their will power?* One of the reasons they failed is because they only committed to *"try"* which is a hedge word that always provides an easy way out when a half-hearted commitment is made. Psychologically, by committing only to *"try"* to do something, you are providing yourself with an easy escape route from your *"pledge"* even before you start. The most difficult things you want to achieve in life are often the hardest to accomplish, which is why unwavering dedication is a requirement from beginning to end.

Time is both your ally and your enemy when trying to break a habit like over-eating, smoking cigarettes, or lack of exercise. One of the more effective ways to break old habits is by employing a twenty-one day personal behavior reconditioning or modification technique like the one I used on my recent and on-going diet. The premise behind this three week behavior reconditioning technique is that an undesired personal habit can be eliminated by replacing it with a more desirable behavior. To cement the new behavior into your daily habits requires practicing it every day for twenty-one days straight. The belief is that once you establish a new routine or habit for twenty-one days, your brain begins to accept and follow a new pattern.

Willpower allows you and I to direct our energy and attention to what we truly care about, whether it's controlling our over-spending, managing our over-eating, or any other bad habit that we know is out of control. There is often a big gap between our thoughts and values; what we want to do, our actions, and what we actually do. This area in between our desired behaviors and our actual behaviors is where our battle for willpower is won or lost. Clearly, it is a battle for self-control that each of us must wage and win in our own minds. This process of reconditioning or reprogramming your own brain for twenty-one days straight is a form of what psychologists call *behavior modification*. It will help you win these battles by strengthening your willpower, making it somewhat easier to adopt the desired changes.

Right after Sheryl and I got married, I decided it was time to stop poisoning her with second hand smoke from my cigarettes. When I finally viewed smoking as my personal enemy, I became motivated to fight and win the smoking battle. Quitting my smoking habit, using the twenty-one day brain reconditioning technique, sounded simple enough and I finally had a good personal reason to quit. I didn't decide to *"try to do it"*; I decided to *"do it"*. There is a big difference between the two. I put a psychological stake in the ground and simply said no more; my addiction to smoking ends here and now. By consciously deciding not to smoke cigarettes for one full day, and then continuing for twenty-one days in a row, I was able to permanently change my behavior. I made a commitment to myself, and to my wife, and then I willed myself to overcome the cravings, bad feelings, and ultimately, the addiction. I can remember the craving caused by the nicotine addiction was still there for a long time, and quitting wasn't easy, but I fought the temptation to smoke minute by minute, hour by hour, and day by day, until I finally eliminated all of my smoking rituals. I could drink a cup of coffee without smoking a cigarette, though the desire was still there, but I had broken my own behavioral pattern. I beat my smoking addiction using this technique 38 years ago and you can do it too!

The twenty-one day behavioral reconditioning technique isn't perfect. It works if you remain disciplined, it doesn't work if you're not. It takes focus and commitment to win these lonely personal self-control battles, which are won or lost one minute, one hour, and one day at a time.

New Twist on Making a New Year's Resolution

In the chapter titled *HEATKTE Key to Success #2*, I reviewed the **Five Step Plan** I developed to get myself back in shape. Here's the true story and the actual results of my diet and exercise plan. Coincidentally, I embarked on this weight-loss program while I was writing this book. My doctor had recommended I increase the amount of exercise I did and lose several pounds, because my cholesterol, blood pressure and pulse rate were too high. My father died when he was only 62 years old as a result of artery blockages, so as a caregiver to two, I knew I needed stay healthy. I made a New Year's Resolution on September 1 to lose fifty pounds by January 1. I went on a healthy diet to get rid of excess pounds, and I started an aggressive exercise program to get myself back in shape.

I started running on my treadmill every other day to accelerate my weight loss program. I posted a motivational quotation on the wall in front of me that I read whenever I need additional inspiration. The quote is about a friend of mine, Gary, who was diagnosed with stage 3 cancer - here's the quote, *"the human spirit always endures, even when the body comes under attack."* I read this quote every time I find myself struggling to finish my run. I think about how Gary has persevered, and how he continues to remain positive, while facing chemotherapy, radiation, surgery, and then even more chemotherapy and radiation. The challenges he faces beating cancer make the challenges I am dealing with seem miniscule in comparison. He has inspired me many mornings to keep running, and I am thankful to him for providing the motivation I need to stay focused on my goal.

With inspiration, desire and a high sense of urgency, my New Year's Resolution to lose fifty pounds by January 1st was accomplished on time as planned! The first question people ask me when they see me is how did you do it? (See the text box for a detailed answer.) Here's the steps I followed to accomplish my goal. It started with an aggressive objective. I then developed a plan which was a series of steps to accomplish the goal. Using a disciplined approach, I executed my plan while tracking my progress in a daily journal. *Goal, plan, execute, track and achieve;* it was as simple as that! Once I completed the first three weeks of my modified diet, the changes became normal parts of my daily and weekly routine. I was never hungry, I ate healthy food, and I felt great! My blood pressure is now normal, I lowered my cholesterol, and my resting pulse rate is 54 beats per minute. Best of all, my doctor took me off my cholesterol lowering medication. I am living proof of the adage, *if one can do it, all can do it!* The achievement of this goal was a result of starting with high expectations, developing a plan of action, and maintaining my commitment for 120 straight days and beyond. Honestly, I believe if I can do it, anyone else with high expectations can do it too!

The Bergdahl "High Expectations" Diet: How I Lost 50 Pounds in Four Months

It started by setting my goal to lose fifty pounds by a targeted completion date, January 1. For me, the key to my 4 month weight loss program was establishing good habits in the first 21 days. Once I changed my eating habits, I saw immediate results. Staying on the diet became a way of life; it took discipline.

I DON'T EAT: bread, potatoes, fried food, pasta, sweets, eggs, butter, fast food, street vendor food. Salads only at restaurants and limited dairy products.

I DO EAT: a high fiber diet: low fat yogurt, boiled chicken, steamed fish, veggies, rice cakes, apples, and salads with low fat dressing. I snack on carrots and plain "air popped" popcorn. I drink black coffee and plenty of water. I also take a daily multi-vitamin.

MY DIET: This is a low fat, restricted carb, low calorie, low sodium, low dairy, low sugar, bland diet.

Month 1 – I followed the diet listed above with no increase in exercise (lost 20 pounds mostly water).

Month 2 – I continued this diet and began walking for 30 minutes every other day (I lost 15 pounds).

Month 3 – I continued this diet and started jogging for 30 minutes every other day (I lost 10 pounds).

Month 4 – I continued this diet and started running for 30 minutes every other day (I lost 5 pounds).

By following this diet and exercise program, I lost 50 pounds in four months!

DISCLAIMER: I am not a dietician, nutritionist, or doctor. I am using my diet for illustration purposes only and I am not recommending this diet to anyone else. Consult your doctor, as I did, before starting any diet or exercise program!

Even with the best of intentions and high expectations, we can sabotage our own success. Think about a time when you decided to pursue an exciting new goal that was left unfulfilled. You start out gung-ho, but as you begin to experience setbacks or obstacles, you find yourself losing momentum, and then your enthusiasm wanes. You question your own judgment, the plan itself, and even your own capabilities. Once you begin to feel defeated, you lose your commitment and whatever momentum you initially created grinds to a halt. You end up giving up before you've really even gotten started. Sadly, even good intending people sometimes *throw in the towel* way too early, quitting on achievable goals, never knowing if they could have succeeded had they persevered. In the final analysis, they fail when they could have triumphed because they really only made a half-hearted commitment. They should have followed the sage advice of Star Wars, Jedi Grand Master Yoda, who challenged his students with the standard, *Do or Not Do... No Try.*

If setting and achieving personal goals was easy, everyone who wanted to lose weight, quit smoking, or start an exercise program, would succeed. That's the reason why most New Year's resolutions fail long before February even arrives.

Effort versus Results

Early in my career, I had a job that required traveling every week to cities in Texas, Louisiana, and Mississippi. I was so busy I really had to focus to stay on top of my job responsibilities. One Wednesday, while I was attending meetings in Harahan, Louisiana, near New Orleans, I received an urgent phone call from my supervisor, Jerry, who worked in Dallas, Texas. After exchanging pleasantries, Jerry asked me a question I will never forget, *"Michael, where is your weekly report?"* My weekly report was due in his office on Monday afternoons each week and it was now

2 days late. I justified the lateness of my weekly report by telling Jerry a number of what I considered valid, travel-related excuses. Jerry listened politely, and when I was finished making my excuses, he asked me once again, in a bone-chilling tone, exactly the same question, *"Michael, where is your weekly report?"*

In that moment, I experienced an epiphany. It was one of those rare, life-changing experiences that happen to each of us when you can point to an exact moment in time when a major change or shift in your thinking has taken place. Up to that point in my life, I had been able to get away with providing weak excuses for my own lack of performance in my dealings with my parents, teachers, and my supervisors; but not with Jerry. He cared enough about me that he refused to let me off the hook. To him, my excuse was an invitation for him to lower his standards, and he would have no part of it. He held me accountable and taught me a lesson that day which I will never forget. Of course, I stopped what I had been doing, prepared my weekly report and sent it to him within the hour after his call.

As I later reflected on what had happened, I realized Jerry had taught me a lesson that I continue to embrace to this day. His intention was positive because he cared about me; his firm guidance was his way of mentoring me. The lesson he was teaching me was to stop making excuses for my lack of performance and start following through 100% of the time on my commitments. He was teaching me the importance of having integrity. From that point onward, I was determined to operate with integrity by living up to my commitments each and every time.

Over the years, like Jerry, I have become hypersensitive to the quality of commitments people make to me. When I hear people say they are going to *try* to do something, I am never confident they will actually follow through and accomplish whatever it is they are *trying* to do. When I have heard my children say they will try to do something, often that try ends up

To really excel, it helps to pursue what you are really interested in, and really good at, with a passion bordering on obsession to be the very best!

unfulfilled. Later, when I follow up with them, they are free to respond, *"No I didn't do it; I told you I would try!"* If you find yourself hedging by saying words like *try, would've, could've, should've, might, or maybe,* stop yourself immediately and make a stronger commitment by saying I will do it or ponder the proactive question: *how can I do it?* Be decisive and go through life unafraid to make solid commitments upon which you actually intend to follow through. Don't live a life of half-hearted promises leaving your personal resume strewn with starts and stops, and unfinished business. Be known by others as someone they can always count on to *operate with integrity.* Most importantly, challenge yourself to always do what you say you will do, when you say you will do it!

Negative Self-Talk

If you find yourself lacking confidence, negativity, begets more negativity, which can lead to a vicious, downward spiral that becomes negatively self-fulfilling. Negativity breeds negative self-talk, which comes out when you affirm your inability with negative thoughts or statements like:

o   I can't do this because . . .

o   I don't have the education required to…

o   I don't know how to…

o   I never was any good at…

o   I am trapped in this miserable job so…

o   That will never work because…

o   I lack the experience required to…

o   I should have known better than to . . .

o   I'm not smart enough to…

- o   I'm destined to fail because...
- o   I am not qualified to...
- o   I don't have the discipline it takes to...
- o   I may as well quit before...
- o   Why do I even try to...

From time to time, we all make damaging negative affirmation statements about ourselves, but when you catch yourself thinking negative thoughts or speaking negatively about your own ability, stop! Negative affirmations indicate a self-confidence problem. If you find you are reinforcing negative beliefs with negative thoughts and statements, you are programming your brain for failure. You know about the power of positive thinking, but there is an equal and opposite power of negative thinking.

Let me illustrate that point with a story about a professional football player. The coach decided to run the ball rather than try to kick a game-winning field goal on fourth down. His team failed to make a first down, and they ended up losing the game. At the news conference after the game, the coach was asked why he hadn't tried to kick a field goal. His response was, "*I didn't believe my kicker would make it!*" The kicker unfortunately overheard what his coach had said, and he was devastated. From that moment onward, that kicker was no longer effective. For the rest of that season, his performance deteriorated, eventually leading to his expulsion from professional football. When the kicker was later asked what had happened to his kicking performance, he said, "*Ever since my coach said he didn't believe I could kick that field goal, I stopped believing in my own ability.*"

The important lesson to take from this story is this: by allowing negative comments made by others to dominate your thinking, you can do damage to your own self-esteem, and your own self-confidence, which can lead you down the path to failure. The good news is that regardless of what negative things others may say about you, you can re-program your own brain to think positively by embracing affirmation statements like these:

- ✓ I know I can do it because…
- ✓ I may not have done this before but . . .
- ✓ I have the experience to…
- ✓ I will work hard to…
- ✓ I have all the knowledge to…
- ✓ I have prepared myself so…
- ✓ I enjoy facing new challenges because…
- ✓ I am well prepared to handle…

You might be thinking how can I possibly use positive affirmations when all I am hearing are negative thoughts and opinions? The quick answer is if you act enthusiastic, you'll be enthusiastic; if you act positive, you'll be positive. That's the great thing about using positive affirmations. If you simply make the choice to think positive thoughts, you have no choice but to become more positive. You can also use the following success affirmation statement I wrote as a positive reinforcement touchstone.

SUCCESS AFFIRMATION

I will dream big dreams, set lofty goals and I will control my own destiny I am willing to take managed risks, challenge the status quo and swim upstream. I will face my fears, and overcome life's obstacles, as I boldly challenge myself to pursue greatness. I will never become complacent and I will not be satisfied with simply maintaining things the way they are. I believe I can always improve upon my best effort! With care and forethought, I will take managed risks. I will study, ask questions, seek advice, challenge conventional wisdom, and overcome obstacles. I will be tireless in my insatiable desire to learn. Fearless, confident, and committed, I will test new ideas knowing some will work and some will not. I will blaze my own trails in a never ending, lifelong-quest, to create my own successful future! I am a dreamer and a visionary who is careful and confident; who's unafraid of change. I truly believe the best in life is yet to come!

You Must Be Willing To Pay the Price

It seems many young people today are determined to get to the top of their profession, and they want to get there now! They look around themselves and realize others did it the hard way by investing decades of their lives to get to the top. On the other hand, they have also seen young *"dot com entrepreneurs"*, who had a good idea and became wealthy, seemingly overnight, without even going to college or after dropping out of college. It is no surprise some think, "W*hy should I struggle for decades to get ahead when I can go for it now?"* One good reason is that statistically, more than 80% of small-business start-ups actually fail! There are no shortcuts. The formula for creating a profitable business venture takes hard work, gaining skills, and becoming an expert in your field, which takes years of patient preparation. You must be willing to build a solid foundation to become an expert in your chosen field. I refer to that strong foundation as building substance. You gain expertise by dedicating yourself to learning and there is no easy way around it.

Over the years, I've worked with people who believed that when they get that next-better job or other great opportunity, only then will they be willing to learn the skills that go along with it. In my experience, that is a strategy that has never worked in the past, and it won't work today. If you aspire to move ahead in life, you must be willing to gain the expertise required by building substantial knowledge in advance of the opportunity. There are many people competing with you who are willing to pay the price by gaining the education, training, skills, and expertise necessary in advance. Heed the achievement advice of Thomas Jefferson, who said, *"If you want something you've never had, you must be willing to do something you've never done."*

One Year of Experience Relived Three Times

Pursue your goals with dogged determination, and a willingness to make the sacrifices necessary in order to succeed.

At what point do you have a right to feel frustrated with your lack of career progression? If you are experiencing frustration with your job, you have a right to question whether it is time to pursue a new challenge. Generally speaking, you should feel good about your current role as long as you feel as if you are continuing to learn. Frustration tends to surface when you feel stagnant. You will find you are happiest in your work as long as you have a balanced relationship with your job; what is referred to as a *symbiotic relationship.* That occurs when you are benefiting your company by doing a good job while you simultaneously gain new skills and knowledge.

Most people become frustrated when their relationship with their job is no longer symbiotic. They find they are continuing to give their company good results; while in return, they receive little back in the form of personal and professional development. The reason for the frustration is the imbalance between the contributions you make to your employer versus the experiential benefits you receive. When you are no longer learning, you begin to relive last year's experiences over and over again. If you've worked in your current job for three years, let's clarify the level of experience you actually have with the answer to this question. *Do you have three distinct years of growth, learning, and challenges in those three years of experience or do you have one year of the same experience relived three times?* If your answer is one year of experience relived three times, you have a right to feel frustrated and even bored with your current job! The next question is this: *What do you intend to do about it?*

Even though you may be unhappy because you are achieving far below your true potential many of your peers are in exactly the same situation. *Knowing that's the case how do you insure your skills and abilities stand out from those of your peers?* You do it by differentiating yourself before the opportunity presents itself. Start by creating a reputation within your peer group of being someone who is an intellectually-curious, continuous learner, known for constantly gaining new knowledge and skills.

I used this strategy effectively when I worked for a major corporation. Here was my strategy. When I was promoted into my first corporate headquarters job, it was no surprise to me, because I had prepared myself in advance. I was interviewed against a slate of quality internal candidates. My advantage in getting selected was no accident. I had taken every available opportunity in my previous role to gain the training, skills, and experience necessary to become the natural choice for the next step in my career. Because I had built a solid foundation by preparing in advance, I knew hands down I was the most qualified internal candidate! By taking the initiative to gain the necessary skills and training ahead of time, you might say, I promoted myself. I made the personal sacrifices to gain the skills in advance with no guarantees a good opportunity would be forthcoming.

To achieve your goals in life takes preparing yourself *in advance* of unknown future opportunities too. You'll be frustrated forever if you wait for others to provide you with the guidance, training, direction or knowledge required for your future success. Whether you like it or not, you must take charge of preparing yourself in advance for those highly competitive future opportunities. You must accept the fact that you are in a competition against other aggressive people with similar goals. The further up life's pyramid you try to climb, the stiffer the competition. Yes, it will take hard work to differentiate yourself from your equally aggressive peers, but it's the only way to insure you're the one who stands out. By focusing on your own personal development today, you can eliminate less aggressive career competition tomorrow. With this strategy you will be among the most qualified candidates when promotional opportunities finally become available.

A Lesson Learned from Nature

There are no awards in life for simply showing up. Accolades are bestowed upon those who actually applied themselves and made a difference.

I've been accused of being a deep thinker who looks for life's lessons in some of life's mundane tasks. Well, here's an example. Each winter, well after the leaves have fallen, I go out into the woods on our farm and cut down dead trees, which Sheryl has already carefully marked with flags tied around their trunks. Using my chainsaw, I cut those dead trees down and turn them into firewood that I stack in neat rows near our house. It may sound counter-intuitive, but there is something truly enjoyable about being in the woods on a cold winter day, working hard and getting some honest exercise, by cutting and splitting a stack of firewood. I guess I inherited my love of the woods and interest in cutting down trees from my Scandinavian ancestors, who were lumberjacks. As in this example, some of the best lessons I've learned about life and living were a result of getting close to nature.

When we first bought our farm, I didn't own, and had never operated a chainsaw. With the amount of brush and dead trees in the woods, learning to operate a chainsaw was a necessity. I must admit I was a bit fearful I'd injure myself, because I had never been taught how to safely operate a chainsaw. Fortunately, a friend who already had the experience taught me how to cut down even large trees in a safe manner. As a result of his tutelage I have now safely cut down more than 100 dead trees over the past 20 years.

Some of the trees I've cut down were more than twenty inches in diameter. Hand splitting large hardwood trees of that size presents a real challenge. Still, I choose to use a maul and muscle to complete the job. With small logs, it is easy, one swing of the maul is often all it takes to split them; large green logs are often far more difficult. When you try to split big logs, it often takes 4 or 5 cracks with the maul before the log will split. Interestingly, it isn't that final swing of the maul that causes a log to split; it is the cumulative impact of the combined effort of many swings of the maul. Occasionally, there are extremely hard logs that, as hard as I try, I can't split. In those cases, I found a trick that works virtually every time; I simply flip the log over and split it from the other side. It's exactly the same log, I just attack it from a different direction, and more often than not, it works!

Chopping down a tree and splitting it into firewood is like the achievement of most of our worthwhile goals in life. It is physically tiring, frustratingly difficult, and mind-numbingly tedious. The accomplishment of challenging tasks takes overcoming initial fears of the unknown, commitment, hard work, patience, and persistence. From my own experience, there are times when you need to simply step back and look at an old problem from an entirely new and different angle to find a solution. As in flipping a log over and splitting it from the other side, the answer to many of the challenges you face may be right in front of you, hidden in plain sight, if you are willing to try different untried approaches to solve the problem.

HEATKTE
(Pronounced: Het-**Ka**-Tee)
Key to Success #5

High Expectations Are The Key To Everything

HEATKTE Keys to Success

KEY #1: VISION & PURPOSE

KEY #2: PLAN & STRATEGIZE

KEY #3: EFFORT & EXECUTION

KEY#4: AFFIRM & BELIEVE

KEY#5: ACHIEVE & SOAR

KEY#6: PERSEVERE & OVERCOME

HEATKTE Key to Success #5

ACHIEVE & SOAR

I will identify my passion, seek out a mentor, and prepare to pursue my dreams.

Do you remember when you were a child being asked, *what do you want to be when you grow up? How did you answer that question? Like so many others, did you aspire to become a fireman, policeman, ballerina, singer, actor, actress or astronaut? What did you actually become when you grew up versus your early dreams?* When Sheryl and I were in college, we both aspired to someday work together as social workers on an American Indian reservation. Our idealism was quickly shattered when we discovered the selection criteria for those jobs included a preference for those who were actually at least partial descendents of American Indians! Many of us have a dream for our lives that has been thwarted for one reason or another. Out of necessity, we ended up going in an entirely different direction for economic reasons or simply because another opportunity came along at a time we needed it. *What happened to our idealism and that passion for what we really wanted to do with our lives? Why have so many of us settled for something less than our dreams?* Surprisingly, the answer may be found by studying basic human nature.

We All Think We are the Best!

Our self-perceptions, aspirations, and the reality of the world around us are rarely aligned by chance. Interestingly, the biggest obstacle each of us faces to actually becoming the best we can be is our inflated self-image.

In our society, everyone thinks they are better than they actually are, and more often than not, our self-image does not always portray reality. What we think is outstanding is really quite average. What we think is average may be borderline acceptable. This deluded way of thinking creates a leveling effect, and if you are not careful, you will become part of a large herd of quite average people, who share the same inflated views of their average abilities. This isn't just an opinion. There are studies that have verified this phenomenon.

In a psychological study conducted by the College Board, a random group of people was asked to rank themselves on *their ability to get along with others*. All of the participants viewed themselves in the top half of the population. Incredibly, sixty percent rated themselves in the top ten percent of the population, and a full twenty five percent thought they were in the top one percent of the population. In a parallel finding, seventy percent rated themselves in the top quartile in *leadership*.

In a similar study by the College Board, nearly a million high school seniors were asked to indicate *"how you feel you compare with other people your own age in several areas of ability"*. Sixty percent reported themselves as better than average in *athletic ability*. In leadership ability, seventy percent rated themselves as above average. In ability to get along with others, zero percent of the respondents rated themselves below average, sixty percent rated themselves in the top ten percentile, and twenty five percent saw themselves among the top one percentile. *So why is it that we all think we are the best? Why is it that we are so wildly irrational about ourselves when it comes to objectively evaluating our own strengths and weaknesses?* Our inaccurate self-perceptions may have something to do with that expression *"fake it until you make it."* It seems to work in real life, just take a look at some of the *successful* people around you like your co-workers and even your current supervisor! You'll find examples of people who have achieved a degree of success, but with that success, they may now be stretched beyond their capabilities. *What causes this to happen and why is it allowed to go on?* The answer may surprise you.

Everybody Reaches Their Level of Incompetence

Decades ago, Dr. Laurence J. Peter first published his oft quoted book, *The Peter Principle*. The premise behind his ground breaking theory is that every employee will rise or get promoted to his or her own level of incompetence. *The Peter Principle* is based on the notion that employees will continue to get promoted as long as they are competent, but at some point they will fail to get promoted beyond a certain job level, because it has become too challenging for them. At that point, Dr. Peter explains, "*they have reached their level of incompetence*". Over time, Dr. Peter believes every position in the organizational pyramid will be filled by someone above you who is not competent enough to carry out his or her new duties. By the way, Dr. Peter was describing people like you and me when he developed *The Peter Principle*, because he believes all of us eventually reach that point! So

All of us share similar dreams for our lives: to reach our full potential, to be rewarded for our contributions, and to make some kind of difference in the world.

knowing that, take an honest look at where you are in your career today because you may have already reached your level of incompetence! Unfortunately, once employees in organizations rise to their level of incompetence, they end up settling in right where they are. I experienced this with several incompetent superiors above me when I worked for some of the largest, most respected companies in the world. I'm sure you've experienced this too. The Peter Principle is a problem for anyone who has high expectations for their own career. This reality is particularly frustrating for those who aspire to climb the corporate career ladder, which is blocked by an incompetent supervisor above them. Incompetent superiors can't do their own job properly let alone help you advance your career. To be honest, they wouldn't help you if they could, because they rely on the good work of capable people like you to make them at least appear to be competent.

If you are in the unenviable position with an incompetent supervisor in control of your career and your future opportunities, you are experiencing an all too common problem. The options are few but there are strategies you should consider. Get to know the managers in positions two or three levels above you in your organization. Your boss's boss has the authority to promote you out of the situation you find yourself in. Be careful to mind corporate politics so you don't get yourself in hot water, and never bad mouth your current supervisor to others in the process. *The Peter Principle* is another important example of why those who strive to be the best must carefully and quietly take control of their own destiny if they expect to move ahead.

Are You Wasting Precious Time Working for Your Current Employer?

There are three very important questions you need to ask yourself, and answer affirmatively, to determine if your current employer, and the supervisor for whom you work, really deserve your unconditional loyalty:

Question #1: *Do they really care about you as a person, not just the quality of your work?*

Question #2: *Are they committed to your personal success, not just the success of the company?*

Question #3: *Have they proven to you that they are really looking out for your career interests?*

Unfortunately, many people answer one or more of these important career questions with a resounding *"NO"*. You're not alone if you believe the best career opportunities aren't at your current workplace. Mike

Myatt, a self-described leadership myth-buster, interviewed countless employees to determine their career-related perceptions, and here's what he discovered:

- More than 30% believe they'll be working someplace else inside of 12 months.
- More than 40% don't respect the person they report to.
- More than 50% say they have different values than their employer.
- More than 60% don't feel their career goals are aligned with their employer's plans.
- More than 70% don't feel appreciated or valued by their employer.

It would appear from these discouraging statistics that *employee loyalty* is an oxymoron. In reality, employees are about as loyal to their companies, as companies are to their employees! Reading these findings, you can't help but conclude that your company's leaders aren't really concerned about your career interests. Think about it this way if you are a career driven individual, *did you ever consider the fact that your supervisor has a vested interest in keeping you right where you are?* If you are a great performer, think about what your supervisor ends up with if you get promoted. They get an open job, along with the necessity to train someone new, plus they lose productivity. Also keep in mind, your current supervisor may make a recommendation on your behalf, but rarely has the authority alone to offer you a promotion - that's not within the scope of their job responsibilities. Don't ever forget, it is the person in the supervisory job two levels above you, who has the authority to promote the brightest people like you. Get to know that individual and make certain they know the quality of your work if you ever expect to move ahead!

One way to establish a long term plan is by working backwards to determine the steps needed between then and now to accomplish your goals.

You have two clear cut career choices. The first is to simply accept your plight and stay right where you are with the knowledge you're going nowhere fast. Lots of people make this choice and your company prefers employees like that. The second, and more desirable choice, is to proactively take control of your own career. Your employer and your supervisor won't like this choice, but it is the only way for you to get ahead on your timetable and maintain your sanity!

Unveiling the Mystery behind How Corporations Evaluate Your Performance

As a Human Resources Executive, I required our company's leadership team to force rank the job performance of all employees, in every department, using a modified bell shaped curve. A typical example of a bell shaped curve of a group of employees using percentages looks like this: 5%, 20%, 50%, 20%, and 5%. We believed that people in our society and the performance of our own employees fell into a similar type of normal distribution pattern. Using these percentages, we created five buckets, for force ranking employee performance evaluations: "A" (5%), "B" (20%), "C" (50%), "D" (20%), and "E" (5%), which we then strictly followed. As an example, if we had 60 employees who were receiving performance reviews, our forced ranking would yield: 3 employees who were "A's", 12 employees who were "B's", 30 employees who were "C's", 12 employees who were "D's", and 3 employees who were "E's". The "A" players were considered our truly outstanding performers, the best of the best, and represented only the top 5% of our employee population. Our very good performers were our "B" players, representing 20% of our employees. Our "C" players were our good or average performers, and 50% of our employees fell into that category. The forth category was our "D" players, who were our fair performing employees; 20% of our employees fell into this category. Finally, we actually recognized 5% as "E" players, who were considered poor or unacceptable performers, who we systematically moved out of the company as quickly as possible! Statistically, we evaluated our employees' performance, using this bell shaped curve, which we felt was a fair representation of our employee population, the people in the work world around us, and the world in general. If you work for an organization, it is likely your performance is measured, evaluated and slotted into a similar normal performance distribution curve whether you like it or not. Think back to the self-perceptions of people from that College Board Study quoted earlier and it is no surprise why employees feel frustrated by this type of performance review system.

No Wonder You Can't Get Ahead

Strive to be known for your integrity by taking personal responsibility when you make a mistake, by apologizing, fixing your mistake, and moving on!

In addition to your annual performance evaluation, it is likely your company also ranks you against your peers, on a separate scale that compares your *promotional potential* to one another. Based on intangible leadership qualities, your promotional potential is force ranked against all other salaried employees, who are your peers in the organization. Your promotional potential is then secretly labeled *top-third, middle-third or bottom-third* based on the opinions of senior leaders who make a subjective evaluation of your *promotability*. The theory behind this ranking is to make certain only those few "A" and "B" players, who are characterized as highly promotable, are on the top third of the list. When it's time to make future promotion decisions, those are the only people selected for serious consideration. If you are not on that *top-third* list, you won't be considered. In many companies, steps are taken to preferentially compensate the *top-third* while also providing them with targeted leadership develop training to enhance their skills, to keep them from leaving. Whether it is fair or not, once your future potential has been labeled *middle-third or bottom-third,* within your peer group, your chances of being promoted are slim to nil. Exclusion from the *top-third* is not limited to just "C", "D" and "E" players; some "A" and "B" players who are on the top of the *performance list* also won't make it on the top-third of the *promotable list* either. *The idea for you to grasp here is that your performance is not synonymous with your potential.* The sad thing for those employees in the *middle-third and bottom-third,* who are doing their best to get promoted, is that employers won't honestly tell you how they perceive your potential. It's like a best kept corporate secret, and because of it, you may end up getting strung along, potentially wasting years of your precious career in an environment with no chance for promotion. In case you ever wondered why you have been passed over for promotional opportunities, this is the reason. Now, at least you understand the reason behind why you are frustrated!

Why Pay Increases Fail to Motivate

When we awarded annual *merit* pay increases, we created a pay increase budget pool. Some years, it was only 2.5%. What this means to all employees is that the "A" players would get 3% increases, the "B" players would get 2.5% increases, and the "C" players would get 2% increases. In this scenario, even if you were an "A" level performer, you would only receive a *"merit"* increase that was 1% more than a "C" level performer! Add to that the fact that the annual cost of living index often rises 2% or more each year and merit increases are effectively neutralized, wiping out any real *merit* pay gains. You know you are caught in the corporate compensation trap when you find yourself fighting for scraps and fretting over whether you'll get a 2%, a 2.5%, or a 3% increase. You will never get ahead financially by receiving small merit increases like these, because with inflation, they are at best equal to cost of living increases.

If you are compensated with this type of carrot and stick performance review system, you know firsthand that small annual *"merit"* pay increases are not a motivator. You may find you are actually de-moralized, insulted, and demotivated each year when you receive your *merit* increase notification from your supervisor. If you are frustrated and even unhappy with this type of pay system, it's understandable. Regardless of how you perform, not only can't you get ahead, you find yourself actually losing ground financially. Think about the negative impact this can have on an organization when the majority of employees become demotivated because they have lost the incentive to perform at the highest level! Performance review and merit pay systems like this are actually quite common in companies across the world. This type of pay plan may make sense to companies trying to plan their payroll budgets but leave a lot to be desired with respect to employee motivation. Unfortunately, due to the flaws in their design, this type of forced ranking performance review system in the end actually breeds mediocrity!

> The fastest way to accelerate your personal development is by asking the experienced people around you to teach you what they know.

I shared this merit pay story with Ben and Amanda who are both high potential people. Ben expressed frustration with the slow progress of his career and confided that he had been passed over recently for a promotional opportunity for which he knew he was the most qualified candidate. I explained to Ben and Amanda the secret to career progression and accelerating their earnings; they must either find the path to move up in their own company, or they must take control of their own careers and move on to another company. This was my personal approach throughout my entire career, which gave me control of my own destiny. Over the years, having changed companies five times, I was able to progress in my career and bump my earnings on each move up by 20% to 30%. Within 6 months of hearing this advice, Ben and Amanda each had found a better job with a new company offering more responsibility, along with 20% pay increases. By discovering this new career reality, they now have taken control of their own destinies forever, and you can do it too.

Most people view themselves as "A" or "B" players when in actuality most human beings fall into the "C" player average category. Whether we care to admit it or not, it's true that most people in our society fit neatly into a normal distribution curve. Of course, everyone would enjoy being recognized as "A" and "B" players, but the reality is that most people in the world are performing at, and deserve to be rewarded at, the "C" level. The bell-shaped performance curve is a harsh reality of life.

The good news is that you can choose to become an "A" or "B" player. You do it by replicating the performance strategies of bona fide "A" players. The bad news is if you continue to use the people around you as your standard of comparison for your performance, you will be setting your performance bar far too low. This approach by design compares your performance to the herd average, which, at best, will allow you to perform at the high end of the "C" player level.

Look around you at the people with whom you come in contact every day. *How many people do you know who are truly driven to become the very best at what they do?* There aren't as many as you might think. It's almost as if there is a herd mentality with the standard of comparison being other members of the same herd of average people. *If your strategy is to do things the same way as everyone around you, how can you expect to achieve excellence?* The truth is that approach won't work and it has never worked. If that is your strategy, I understand why you feel frustrated by your inability to rise above your peers. Don't allow yourself to get bogged down in the mire of mediocrity that surrounds you! Change your approach and choose to be different by breaking free of the herd mentality!

The best athletes, sports teams, business leaders, corporations, teachers, top students, outstanding professors, research scientists, doctors, and great universities all use the top performers in their field as their standard of comparison. They don't select the middle of the pack as their benchmark, because they know if they do, they too will achieve similar average results. They compare themselves to the best of the best in their field. By setting the bar high, they guarantee their own performance will always be among the very best.

The Herd Average: The Best Compared To What?

Here is an illustration of the herd average that captures the concept of the *top-third, middle-third and bottom-third as it relates to performance and potential.* If you were told there was a baseball player standing behind a curtain, and that player is wearing a baseball uniform, a baseball hat, baseball shoes, and carrying a baseball glove, you would agree that accurately describes a baseball player. If you were told this player plays baseball at an *outstanding level,* the question you should be asking is: *outstanding compared to wha*t? When the player steps out from behind the curtain, standing before you is a 12-year-old, truly outstanding, little league baseball player. Obviously, there is a big difference between an outstanding big league player, minor league player, college player, high school player, pony league player, and a little league baseball player. This illustration is analogous to what happens when you compare your performance and potential to the people around you. Are you comparing your performance to a *"little league"* peer group or to a group of *"big league players?"*

If you think you're the best at what you do, the question remains: *the best compared to what? At what level are you trying to achieve? In your mind, who is your standard of comparison?* You may be outstanding compared to the peer group around you today but what about if you compared yourself to others who are striving to be the best in a similar job across your industry locally, nationally or even around the world? In business, often

Success is one part vision and one part inspiration, with equal parts: planning, prioritization, and superior execution.

when a company CEO is asked to judge the strength of his/her own top leadership team, each will proudly point to several key executives whom they characterize as outstanding "A" players. Often, what that CEO has done is simply identify the best of his/her own staff. To use a politically incorrect phrase used by headhunting experts, *the CEO has identified the tallest midgets.* The peer group used for the comparison is not necessarily the brightest or the best; so to be outstanding amongst a peer group of average performing people is not that hard, and in truth, it may not be saying very much. If you are in this situation, and you are striving to be the best, you must look outside your own peer group for higher standards of comparison to truly excel.

It's Hard to Soar Like an Eagle...

There is a fable about an eagle that further illustrates the influence your peer group can have over you and your performance. It offers a great lesson about how an eagle, raised in a flock of chickens, becomes conditioned by its peers, and begins to act like a chicken. Here is that fable called T*he Eagle and the Chickens:*

Once upon a time… there was an eagle that fell from the safety of his nest to the ground below. A chicken farmer found the baby eagle, brought it to his farm, and raised it in a chicken coop amongst his flock of chickens. The eagle was accepted by the chickens as one of their own. The eagle grew up doing what chickens do, living like a chicken, and believing in his mind that he was a chicken.

The ornithologist from the local zoo visited the chicken farm to see if what he had heard about an eagle, acting like a chicken, was really true. He knew this great bird had far more potential than its current peer group allowed. The eagle had obviously adapted to its surroundings and was indeed acting like a chicken. An eagle is born to soar fearlessly across the sky, the ornithologist thought, and nothing can change that; but still, here is an eagle choosing to achieve far below its full potential.

He lifted the eagle above his head and said, "Eagle, stretch your wings and soar into the sky where you belong." The eagle promptly dropped to the ground and continued doing what captive chickens do. The chicken farmer proudly proclaimed, "I told you that eagle thinks and acts like a chicken."

The ornithologist returned the next day and tried again. He took the eagle to the top of the barn and said, "Eagle, you belong in the sky, not on the ground, so fly away." The eagle once again decided to rejoin its fellow chickens by fluttering its wings as it dropped down to the barnyard below.

Frustrated, the ornithologist asked the farmer to let him try one more time. The next day, the ornithologist and the farmer took the eagle to the peak of a nearby mountain. They were far enough away that the eagle could not see the farm or the chicken coop from its secluded mountain perch. The ornithologist held the eagle above his head, pointed to the sky and said, "You may think you are a chicken, but you have the heart of an eagle. Your destiny is to soar across the sky high above the earth, so spread your wings and fly." This time the eagle finally understood as it spread its massive wings, and soared into the sky.

Like the eagle in this fable, reaching your full potential and achieving at the highest level starts with a choice to get out of the comfort zone created by your existing peer group. You must stop comparing your performance to the mostly average people around you, or you are destined to become average at best. You must be willing to do what the others around you are unwilling, unable, or incapable of doing to give yourself a chance of realizing your full potential. Now's the time for you to release your inner eagle, so you can start soaring above your peers.

Choose to do what others won't do to get ahead

When I was growing up, my father moved our family from city to city every time he was promoted by his employer. I changed schools every few years and as a result I was forced to build new friendships. When you are the new kid on the block, one of the best ways I always found for making new friends is by playing sports. I was always extremely competitive, I was a good athlete, and I loved all kinds of sports. I could shoot hoops, swing a bat, and catch a pass as well as anybody my age. My strategy each time my family moved was to gain initial acceptance by the kids in my new neighborhood by showcasing my athletic ability, and it worked every time. Interestingly, the first time they met me, I would always get picked last for the team. Once they saw how well I played, the next time teams were selected, I would always be among the first chosen! When I went to college, my love of sports and my athleticism once again helped me make a smooth transition, and allowed me to soar above the rest of my peers.

Mentoring someone else is one of the most gratifying things you can do, so pay it forward by sharing your expertise with others!

When I arrived on campus that freshman year, I immediately tried out for my college soccer team. My initial goal was simply to make the team. I remember there were many freshmen competing for the few slots available for freshman to start on the varsity squad. With so many skilled players trying out for the team, I knew I was going to have to do some-thing really special if I hoped to attract the coach's attention. I decided to differentiate myself from my fellow competitors by developing a strategy and executing it at every practice. My plan was actually quite ingenious; I simply planned to out-work and out-perform my peers. Here's what I did. At the beginning of each and every practice, our coach, who was a real stickler for fitness, made us run ten laps around the track as a warm up; the distance was 2½ miles. I decided from the very first practice to run those laps faster than anyone else. Picture twenty-five players jogging those laps clumped together and me running those laps as fast as I could to break away from the pack. Each day, my goal was to run fast enough to lap the entire team before they completed their ten laps, which is exactly what I did. Amazingly, not one of my peers took up my challenge. My coach took notice from the very first practice and even asked me if I had run track in high school. When the coach later announced the names of the few freshmen who had made the team, my name was one of them. Not only did I make the team, but I was a starter in every game my freshman year. My coach was so impressed with my leadership by example that he selected me to be captain of the team the following year.

I learned that by choosing to make the effort that others are unwilling to make, you not only stand out when compared to your peers, but you rise above them. My commitment to making the team is an example of *what I thought about most of the time is what I would become.* I envisioned what it would take to make the team and I went out and executed a foolproof plan. Success in business, sports, and in life is about taking initiative, making the right choices, and being willing to make the sacrifices that others won't make. You can choose to exert the effort it takes to be the best you can be, or you can choose to be just an average member of the herd. In the end, the choice is yours. The simple truth is: *hard work and dedication are rewarded in the end.*

Creating Distance between Yourself and the Rest of Your Competition

One of the most common approaches company leaders use to differentiate their organizations from those of their competitors is by benchmarking their own best practices against those of other great organizations. Many of the most successful companies in the world routinely meet with the executives from other companies from inside and outside their own industry to learn new and better methods for improving their operations. Benchmarking best practices against the best companies is one of the strategies great companies use to create competitive distance between themselves and the rest of their competition.

It's akin to the concept of a breakaway in the Tour de France bicycle race. A small team of 3-5 bicycle riders breaks away from the main peloton of more than 100 riders. In a break away, this small group of riders works together as a team to create distance between themselves and the rest of the pack of bicycle riders. By constantly rotating the lead position, the energy of each individual breakaway team member is conserved, allowing them to go faster than they possibly could individually. By taking advantage of the synergy created by the breakaway team, the entire group creates separation between themselves and the rest of the competitors.

If you were told you could adopt a similar strategy as an individual, would you be willing to give it a try? You really can use a personal strategy like benchmarking to accelerate your self-development. It is as simple as identifying like-minded individuals, who are similarly driven, and meeting with them by phone or face-to-face periodically to discuss ideas for addressing their challenges and yours. The synergy created will allow both of you to move faster in the direction of your goals, than you could alone.

Emulate the Traits of People around You

Virtually everyone we meet has something to teach us if we are smart enough to figure out what that something is. *Did you ever admire someone because they had strong interpersonal skills, had a great sense of humor, or because they were a great leader?* If you see traits in others you admire, you can emulate those traits and make them your own. It's true. One of the best ways to self-develop your personal skill set is by copying or emulating the desirable traits of others. You can improve your speaking skills, ability to carry on fulfilling conversations, and even your leadership skills, by copying the behaviors of those who are already skilled in those areas. Try it. It really works!

Parents are the Best Mentors

The definition of *"mentor"* is someone who acts as a counselor, advisor, teacher, or guide, who can be trusted to look out for your best interests. Based on that definition, it was my parents who served as my first mentors. They taught me right from wrong, instilled my work ethic, and gave me the space I needed to grow as an individual. It was my parents who also planted the original seeds that germinated into who I am in my career today. My father was my first speaking mentor, and my mother was my first writing mentor. My dad thoroughly enjoyed every opportunity he had to speak at company meetings, Lions Club Dinners and Rotary Club Luncheons. My mother was a prolific writer who wrote a

People who have developed expertise are often great teachers willing to share their knowledge and experience with others.

newspaper column for many years. As my earliest mentors, they shared their knowledge, experience, and expertise with me, which encouraged me to develop my speaking and writing skills. In turn, I have passed the Bergdahl writing and speaking genes on to my son and daughter. Both have already written articles which were published in magazines, and each of them is an aspiring, fearless public speaker. I give a great deal of credit to both of my parents for the profound influence they had on the direction my life has taken. Someday, we hope our children will feel the same way about us!

Just like my parents guided me, I'm sure your parents provided guidance and direction to you. Many people give credit to their parents for instilling the right values and for providing the initial foundation upon which their future accomplishments were built. As most parents do, my wife and I have always tried to act as mentors to our children. Sometimes, parents wonder if their mentoring messages are getting through to the young people they so much want to help. All of us as adults continue to be influenced by the instruction and expertise we learned long ago from our parents, grandparents, and other influential adults. We don't realize those seeds were being planted at the time. Parents begin providing mentorship to their own children starting at an early age. Having strong influential role models, who set the right example, is critical to young people, who are just starting out in their lives.

I must admit, in my parental mentoring experience, my own children have not always been the most willing protégés. A good example of my mentoring failings comes from the time our son Paul was learning to drive. I assumed I was the perfect driving instructor, since I have decades of driving experience. After the first driving lesson, Paul said, "*Dad, you may be great at other things, but you are a lousy driving teacher! I've watched you drive, and you're a terrible driver!*" If that wasn't enough, he reminded me that I had instructed our daughter, Heather, how to drive, and as a result, she became an extremely aggressive driver who had three minor car accidents as a teenager. Paul was right about my driving, and he is right about the results of the driving instruction I had given to his sister. My frustration shows when I get behind the wheel and I must have taught those same aggressive tendencies to Heather! We all agreed the best solution was to find Paul a professional driving instructor who had the patience, skills, and teaching experience necessary to build his self-confidence behind the wheel.

The moral of this story is that if you are looking for a mentor to help you, be sure to find someone who has the patience, experience, and the actual ability to teach the skills you need. As in my example of trying to teach Paul to drive, don't assume just because a potential mentor has the experience you are seeking that they have the ability to teach those skills to you. That day, Paul taught us an unforgettable lesson: *we all need to choose our mentors wisely!*

Find a Mentor, Be a Mentor

Mentors bring a wealth of experience, and most can teach you the secrets they learned the hard way. By listening to their sage advice, you can avoid embarrassing and costly mistakes, learn more quickly, and make better choices the first time. The best case mentoring scenario is when the relationship is symbiotic, and both the mentor and protégé are growing as a result of learning from one another.

With the help and support of my wife, my parents and my mentors, I have become a successful international speaker who has spoken professionally in cities on six continents. I have also authored six books. I could not have done any of it without the guidance and support I received over the years from my many mentors. I can name more than 30 mentors, both women and men, who have positively influenced my life by sharing valuable life lessons with me. As you might expect, a few of my mentors are younger than I; some are my age, and quite a few are older. I have mentors who influenced me for a short period of time and moved on, while others have remained constant in my life. Mentors taught me lessons that I still embrace and share with others. Here are several examples:

➢ Don't focus on what you can't do; focus on what you can do.
➢ The most important skill is the ability to present your ideas to others.
➢ Don't make excuses or accept excuses from others.
➢ Invest as much energy in your family as you invest in your work.
➢ No matter what you do, strive to be the best.

➢ If you are willing to work hard, you can overcome any adversity.

➢ Don't be afraid to lean on others for emotional support in tough times.

➢ Trust in your own capability; try to do what you've never done before.

➢ Find your unique niche and you can make a difference in the world.

➢ Do what others aren't willing to do to catapult yourself to the next level.

➢ Find a way to pursue the dream that's planted in your heart.

➢ Each and every one of us can choose to make a difference in the world.

➢ Don't make the mistake of allowing others to control your dreams.

➢ First impressions are critical in this world.

➢ Sources of inspiration are all around us.

➢ Believe in others even more than they believe in themselves.

➢ The only limits are those you choose to set for yourself.

➢ When you love what you do, it shows.

Some of the life lessons listed above are pretty simple, while others have the potential to be life-changing. (A complete list of my mentors and their lessons can be found in the Appendix in the back of this book.) There are many experts and gurus all around you who would be happy to share their knowledge and experience with you. All you need to do is ask for help, and more often than not, they'll agree to assist you.

Giving back to others... paying it forward

One of our goals for this book was to provide life lessons to our son and daughter. It is our way of paying it forward. In my role as a parent and mentor, I tried all kinds of approaches to guiding and teaching my own children. As they got older, the methods I tried were even more creative. Based on my own life experience, I developed the following mentoring life lessons checklist as a touchstone for living, or a directional life compass, designed to help get them on track and keep them on course. I call it, *Are You Ship Shape?*

- ✓ Apprenticeship –Work with and learn from experts who are willing to teach you their craft
- ✓ Friendship – Develop an inner circle of 2 or 3 great friends
- ✓ Citizenship – Be a good neighbor and an asset to your community
- ✓ Ownership – Take responsibility for your own future
- ✓ Penmanship – Show your pride by writing legibly
- ✓ Relationship – Be known as someone who is fair, honest and caring
- ✓ Scholarship – Become a lifelong learner
- ✓ Workmanship – Do every assignment to the best of your ability
- ✓ Salesmanship – Market YOU, your skills and your abilities
- ✓ Hardship – Expect difficulties, persevere and triumph
- ✓ Leadership – Don't wait for direction. Take charge and choose to lead
- ✓ Entrepreneurship – Control your own destiny, be decisive and take managed risks
- ✓ Partnership – Affiliate with like-minded, goal-oriented individuals
- ✓ Kinship – In good times and bad times, your family will always be there
- ✓ Membership – Join organizations that enhance your expertise
- ✓ Fellowship – Build a strong network of people you can count on and trust
- ✓ Worship – Embrace your faith in good and bad times
- ✓ Showmanship – Go out each day and enthusiastically prove what you can do
- ✓ Stewardship – Consciously do what you can to make the world around you a better place
- ✓ Mentorship – Give back by teaching your knowledge and experience to others

My goal as a mentor to my protégées is to impart simple, actionable life strategies. This list focuses on values, believing in your own ability, and taking the bull by the horns. These are self-development life lessons which are tools that provide clear direction on the path to achieving high expectations in everything you do. I really do believe in mentoring and that when the student is ready, the teacher will appear. But remember: a healthy mentoring relationship cannot take place without a willing protégé. Open your eyes, your ears and your heart: your mentors are all around you and they're ready to help. Those potential mentors can lead the proverbial horse to water but they can't make it drink. It's up to you to seek out and use their guidance. You never know who will become your mentors in life and you can't always predict those for whom you will become a mentor. When it happens, I believe it happens for a reason! Always be on the lookout for opportunities to help others and always remain receptive to others who might be willing to help you

When someone does a good deed for you, helps you, or teaches you, instead of paying them back, pay it forward by doing a good deed for someone else. Paying it forward is a selfless act of kindness with no expectation of remuneration or reciprocation. When you help others, you are making a difference in the world, and you are leaving a legacy. It's a win/win scenario for you and for those you've helped. As Zig Ziglar once said, *"You can have everything you want in life, if you'll just help enough other people get what they want."* It may sound counterintuitive, but by helping others reach their goals, you'll actually enhance your chances of reaching yours too!

HEATKTE
(Pronounced: Het-**Ka**-Tee)
Key to Success #6

High Expectations Are The Key To Everything

HEATKTE Keys to Success

KEY #1: VISION & PURPOSE

KEY #2: PLAN & STRATEGIZE

KEY #3: EFFORT & EXECUTION

KEY#4: AFFIRM & BELIEVE

KEY#5: ACHIEVE & SOAR

KEY#6: PERSEVERE & OVERCOME

HEATKTE Key to Success #6

PERSEVERE & OVERCOME

I will aggressively take on every obstacle, and no matter what happens, I will not give up until I succeed.

When Sheryl was hospitalized, it was the first time in our married lives that I was solely responsible for taking care of our children. At first, I was overwhelmed by all of my new responsibilities. How would I take care of the children, earn an income, take care of our home, and care for my wife? The only thing I knew for certain was that things as we had known them had changed forever. All the neat and tidy order in our lives was gone. I didn't know until after her stroke that I had the easy job going out to earn a living every day. For the entire time we had been married I had taken the things Sheryl had done for granted! Now, I needed to step up and be a better father and a better husband than I had ever been before. Filling her shoes was impossible, because she is a great mother, who always made our lives so comfortable. Initially, I was intimidated and my confidence was shaken, questioning my ability to deal with the new responsibilities that had been thrust upon me.

Someone once said, adversity can draw a family closer together or tear it apart. Our family was about to experience that old adage firsthand due to the incredible pressure a devastating medical situation places on every member of a family. There is nothing that can prepare you for something like this, and there is no way to know how you'll respond. This was a moment of truth for our family, and I was determined to do everything in my power to hold our family together. Sheryl had survived, I was focused, and our family was committed to persevere; but still the reality of our circumstances would test the strength of our family's collective character.

Initially, one of the biggest challenges I dreaded most was simply how to tell Heather and Paul that their mother had a stroke, that she was in a coma. I couldn't even bring myself to take them to the hospital's intensive care unit to visit their mother because I was afraid the image of her lying there in a coma, totally unresponsive, hooked up to IV's, a catheter, and a ventilator would be forever etched in their young minds. I didn't want them to worry unnecessarily about the unknown and what bad things might happen next to their mother. I waited ten days to tell them the truth, but not until Sheryl was brought out of her medically induced coma. Those were the toughest ten days of our lives! It was only when I knew she was responsive and had all of her mental faculties that I finally took Heather and Paul to the hospital to see their mom for the first time.

Everybody's Got Something... What Have You Got?

I asked Sheryl how she maintained such a positive attitude after having a devastating physical disability thrust upon her at such a young age. Previously, she had full use of both hands and legs, and now, the stroke had permanently paralyzed her right arm, hand and leg. Sheryl had been right-handed and was now forced to relearn skills we all take for granted. She had to learn to write, eat, and even brush her teeth using her left hand. She had to learn to walk again. Imagine how frustrating that must be! So, *how had she stayed so positive through it all?* Sheryl's response will give you insight into her character. She said, *"What choice do I have? I can let this bring me down, or I can thank God for what I can do. When you come close to the end of your life, and you're given a second chance, you* appreciate all the things you have *more than ever before."* What she said next, I'll never forget. She said,

> The possibilities for your life are endless; your only limitations are your self-imposed beliefs.

"Besides everybody's got something! There isn't anyone alive who doesn't face adversity in their life, problems with their job, issues within their family, or even disabilities that are far worse than mine. So, everybody's got something to deal with, and my something just happens to be a stroke."

Her insights stopped me in my tracks. I experienced another life-changing, significant emotional event. You know, Sheryl is right! We all face adversity, and we have people close to us who are also struggling with all kinds of problems. As an example, the members of our large, extended family would be perceived on average as typical when compared to most families. Many of our family members have good jobs, are generally healthy, and they have a positive outlook on life. We also have examples of extended family members, suffering from some kind of physical or mental disability or serious health problems; some, who are unemployed, a few, who are underemployed; some, who have financial problems; a couple, who are on the dole who have simply given up; several who had failed marriages; and a couple, who are downright unhappy for no apparent reason! I really don't think our family is all that different. We all face challenges, issues, problems, and obstacles in our lives. Sheryl got it right when she said, *"We all face some kind of adversity in life, so what are you doing to rise above it?"*

Even Famous People Face Adversity

Can you imagine someone, who is hearing impaired becoming an acclaimed actress? Well, Marlee Matlin did just that. As a result of her portrayal of a deaf student in Children of a Lesser God, Marlee won the Oscar for Best Actress. Her work in film and television earned her a number of prestigious awards. And, consider two extremely famous recording and performing artists, who lost their sight — Stevie Wonder and Andrea Bocelli. Blind from infancy, Stevie Wonder is a leading singer-songwriter, multi-instrumentalist, and record producer. Andrea Bocelli became completely blind as a child, following a sports related injury. He has emerged as one of the world's greatest singing talents, whose albums have sold in the millions around the world. The success enjoyed by Marlee Matlin, Stevie Wonder, and Andrea Bocelli is proof that one can achieve greatness despite profound disabilities such as deafness and blindness.

Many other celebrities have had to overcome adversities of a different order before they were able to achieve the fame for which they are known today. Danny Glover, best known for his starring roles in the blockbuster series Lethal Weapon, was deemed *"mentally slow"* by school authorities before it was determined he was dyslexic. And, Leonardo DiCaprio, the famous film actor, and David Beckham, the soccer star, both suffer from Obsessive Compulsive Disorder. DiCaprio has to force himself not to step on every chewing gum stain on the sidewalk, and he fights the urge to walk through a doorway several times. Beckham is constantly concerned about cleanliness and perfection; anything out of order must be attended to immediately.

Countless individuals in the business world had to overcome a wide range of adversities along the way before they reached the pinnacle. School was a nightmare for Richard Branson due to his dyslexia. Despite his poor academic record, Branson went on to become one of the most imaginative and successful global entrepreneurs, best known for his Virgin Company brand comprised of more than a hundred companies.

Lessons Learned From Life's Challenges

When bad things happen to good people, there is almost always something positive that can be gleaned. If nothing else, valuable lessons can be learned about your own capacity for dealing with life's hurdles. Even as my family went through months of turmoil, I learned several valuable lessons as a result of staring adversity squarely in the eye. I learned that you must believe things are going to get better even when they seem the worst. Though it is difficult, I realized tough decisions must still be made even when I was feeling completely overwhelmed. For this reason, I learned to focus on accomplishing small goals to build my confidence. Unlike any other time in my life, I found myself seeking emotional support from others, which helped me improve my emotional and mental health as well as my outlook. I also embraced my religious faith, and by doing so, I found peace of mind and clarity of direction. Surprisingly, I used adversity as a cause to be overcome which actually made it a source of inspiration. Most importantly, I learned I would not succumb to negative feelings no matter how bad things might get. Good things do come out of bad situations and I found remaining optimistic, decisive, and determined provided the solid foundation I needed for achieving a positive outcome.

Life is a never-ending succession of big and small problems, so you may as well get used to it! You will face problems, seemingly insurmountable obstacles, and heartbreaking challenges that will leave you wondering *why me?* The reality of life is that we are not alone in tackling life's struggles. *We all face adversity in our lives, and the critical question is: how does each of us respond?* In that darkest hour, when you are totally overwhelmed, and certain you lack the capacity to overcome a monumental challenge, don't get bitter, wallow in self-pity and act like a victim! Rise up enthusiastically and face your challenges in life, believing you'll be victorious! Here's a parable called, *Never Give Up, Shake It Off & Take a Step Up,* that illustrates this point.

One day a farmer's donkey fell down into a well. The animal cried desperately for hours as the farmer tried to figure out what to do. Finally, he decided that because the donkey was very old, and the well needed to be covered up anyway, it just wasn't worth the trouble it would take to retrieve the donkey.

He invited all his neighbors to come over and help him fill in the well. Everyone grabbed a shovel and began to shovel dirt. At first the donkey panicked and cried uncontrollably. Then, to everyone's amazement, the donkey quieted down.

After some time, the farmer looked down into the well and he was astonished at what he saw. With each shovel of dirt that hit his back, the donkey was doing something amazing; he was shaking it off and taking a step up.

As the farmer's neighbors continued to shovel dirt into the well on top of the donkey, he would shake it off and take a step up. Pretty soon, everyone was amazed as the donkey stepped up over the edge of the well and happily trotted off.

MORAL OF THE STORY: Life is going to shovel all kinds of dirt on you. The trick to getting out of the hole you are in is to shake it off and take a step up. Each of our troubles is a stepping stone we can use to get out of the deepest holes we find ourselves are in by not stopping, never giving up, shaking it off, and taking a step up.

Facing Adversity

When our son, Paul, was an infant, we noticed he was inattentive when we tried to communicate with him, especially when we spoke to him from behind. For this reason, we decided to take him to Children's Hospital - a four-and-a-half-hour drive from our home - to have the medical staff evaluate him. We spent an entire day with different specialists who, amongst other tests, performed an MRI and an EKG. The focus of concern centered around Paul's ability to hear, so the doctors also decided to give Paul an audiometric examination in a massive hearing booth which was painted to look like a big, yellow school bus, so it wouldn't frighten the children.

Performing at a good, very good, or excellent level is a choice each of us makes each day. Choose to be outstanding!

For an infant, like Paul, to receive an audiometric test, I had to sit in the hearing booth with him, holding him in my lap while the technicians performed the test. The way the hearing test works for infants is actually quite ingenious. The technician introduces sounds into the sealed hearing booth at a series of sound frequencies, one at a time, from very low to very high. As each sound frequency is tested, the technician slowly raises the decibel level coming out of speakers located in front of the child in the top right and top left corner of the darkened hearing booth. As the sound is slowly rising from one or the other speaker (never both), the child eventually looks in the direction of the sound, indicating the sound was actually heard. The moment the child indicates hearing the sound, by glancing in the direction of the speaker, the technician flips on a light above that speaker, and a stuffed monkey is revealed, clapping a pair of cymbals in its hands to reward the child for looking in the correct direction. Conditioning of the child is instantaneous as the child now understands and concentrates to hear the sound to be rewarded by a monkey clapping its cymbals.

As I think back, I remember sitting there with Paul wishing he would hear any of the sounds so that one of those darn monkeys would clap its cymbals, but nothing happened. At frequency after frequency, the decibel level rose to 100 decibels and beyond. The floor was vibrating under my feet from the intensity of the sound waves, and Paul never reacted to a single sound. It was in that moment, that I came to the realization that Paul was profoundly deaf, and Sheryl and I were devastated.

Sheryl cried for most of the four-and-a-half-hour drive back to our home. Miraculously, the next day, she stopped mourning Paul's hearing loss and immediately started proactively searching for solutions. In the days, weeks and months that followed, Sheryl began her personal quest to become an expert in the issues surrounding deaf education. She identified community resources, spoke with educators, and talked with other parents of deaf children. She identified a sign language instructor and arranged to have our entire family trained in sign language. For several years, Sheryl volunteered in a classroom dedicated to the education of the deaf and hard of hearing to learn the best techniques for educating Paul. We were both determined to do everything possible to help Paul reach his full potential.

Hear No Evil

Paul was born into a world that is different from yours and mine. In his non-hearing world, there is no sound. For this reason, in those first highly impressionable early years of his life, he never learned the negative subtleties of the world around him that are learned by the children of the hearing world. Here are some of the subtle and not so subtle differences in Paul's silent world:

- He didn't learn to be afraid of senseless things that other kids were taught to fear.
- He wasn't taught to cry by parents, who shrieked when he fell, as he learned to walk.
- He didn't hear the barrage of "*no's*" each of us hears in a world intent on forcing us to conform.
- He wasn't afraid to play in the basement unaware of the goblins most kids were taught are down there.
- He's not afraid of being judged by others when he expresses himself creatively.
- He's both comfortable and confident when left alone to entertain himself.
- He expresses his true feelings even when it may make others uncomfortable.
- He doesn't worry about wearing the right clothes and saying the right things.

- He doesn't judge those around him based on what they wear or how they look.
- He loves to learn and enjoys getting lost in the story of a good book.
- He's not aware of the latest gossip about who is supposed to be cool and who is not.
- He doesn't have an *"oh woe is me"* outlook in life; he has a *"can do"* attitude.
- He didn't need to be told to do his homework, and he doesn't want anyone else's help.
- He does his chores with little fanfare, because he knows that's his job.
- He believes in himself and his ability to overcome obstacles.
- He's an active participant in life, who gets up early, and stays up late, living each day to its fullest.
- He is his own person, unencumbered by the peer pressures to conform that the rest of us experience.
- He doesn't care what others think about him. He is comfortable *"in his own skin"*.
- He's enabled in a world that views his hearing disability as a handicap.
- He experiences the world in a different way then you and I; he hears no evil.

In many ways, Paul's disability has worked to his advantage, because he wasn't conditioned by society the same way as the rest of us. He has a unique perspective on many things based on his own untainted interpretation of the facts. You will never win an argument with him by telling him everybody thinks this way or does things that way. He will stand his ground, and he can only be convinced his way of thinking is wrong if the facts you present are undeniable. He makes those around him better thinkers by challenging their often shallow opinions of the issues and poor command of the facts. Paul is an inspiration to others, because it is clear he has refused to let his hearing impairment define him as a person, and he has refused to let it disable him. It took us time to realize Paul's hearing impairment is actually a blessing in disguise.

When the going gets tough...

There have been times when the struggles we have faced as a family seemed more than we could endure. In those times, we gathered strength from this inspirational verse called *The Victor* by W.C. Longenecker. You too may find these words helpful as you confront challenges on your journey in life.

If you think you're beaten, you are;
If you think you dare not, you don't;
If you'd like to win, but you think you can't
It's almost certain you won't.
If you think you'll lose, you've lost;
For out in the world we find
Success begins with a person's will
It's all in the state of mind.
If you think you're outclassed, you are;
You've got to think high to rise.
You've got to be sure of yourself
Before you can ever win the prize.
Life's battles don't always go
To the stronger woman or man,
But sooner or later he or she who wins
Is the one who thinks they can.

Don't get bogged down when you experience a setback; learn from your mistakes, adjust your strategy and move forward.

Over the years we have known and admired many caregivers who have shared their stories of hope and inspiration with us. We learned from them that in the most difficult times in your life, you have two choices. You can give up or you can make the best of a bad situation. You can remain strong, or you can allow circumstances outside your control to tear you apart. When Paul's deafness was diagnosed, we had no other choice but to commit ourselves to helping him succeed. We adopted a can-do attitude when at times we felt beaten down. Even in the worst of times, we realized if you cling to the belief that you can overcome whatever challenges you face, you will. It's actually quite easy to give up when you're facing overwhelming challenges, obstacles or problems. Sheryl and I know that feeling, and every time we felt overwhelmed we persevered because we had no other choice. We each adopted the mindset, *failure is not an option.* So even when the odds are stacked against you, keep fighting; you must continue to believe you will succeed regardless of how dire your circumstances may appear. We embraced the following beliefs as we faced adversity, and you may want to consider embracing them as you face life's struggles too.

Believe things are going to get better.

When things seem the worst, having a clear head to focus on solutions is the most difficult but it is also the time when it is most critical. Ask questions like: *Is there anything I can do right now that will make a positive difference? Are there actions I should take today that will improve the situation tomorrow?* Even if you're not feeling particularly optimistic, the simple process of thinking about possible positive solutions will remove your focus from thoughts of the dire circumstances you're in. Once you stop worrying about the worst case scenario, you can think with a clearer mind as you start working through solutions to your problems.

Seek help to improve your emotional health.

Don't be afraid to seek out the help and advice of others. When asked to help, most people are only too happy to lend assistance. You'll be relieved to get emotional support from someone else, who may have already walked in your shoes. I sought support from my older sister who was happy to provide emotional support during the toughest times. If you'll just ask for help, you'll find family members or friends are willing to support you as well.

Embrace your faith.

Do you find yourself wondering whether or not you have what the strength to take on the difficulties you face in life? It is important for you to know there is no adversity you will face in life that you do not already have the capacity within you to deal with. I also learned that I am never totally alone because in the toughest times I have always embraced my faith. When Sheryl suffered her stroke and when we found out Paul was profoundly deaf, I prayed for divine intervention. Each time I asked for help I found my burden was uplifted. Embracing my faith helped got me through those difficult times. If you'll embrace your faith it will get you through the tough times too. Remember this: *if you'll feed your faith as you experience difficult challenges in life, your fears will starve to death.*

Use adversity as a source of inspiration.

When you take inspiration from the adversity you face, you are turning your problems into positive opportunities. You should anticipate life's challenges, and when they crop up, be prepared to proactively deal with them. Ironically, you will grow and learn more as a person from the adversity you face in life than you will from your accomplishments.

Rely on your untapped energy reserves.

Interestingly, in facing the most significant issues in life, regardless of whether you're young or old, you always have a pool of reserve energy to tap into when you need it most. You can stretch your days to eighteen hours if need be for days on end, and your energy reserve and adrenaline will kick in to keep you going! I am not sure where it comes from, but you will find you do have a bottomless pool of energy to tap into when you need it most.

Refuse to give up, no matter how bad things get.

Think back to all of the seemingly insurmountable problems you have worked through in your life that are now only distant memories. You could have given up, but you didn't. Strong people always survive tough times. Remain committed to do whatever it takes, for as long as it takes, and you will never be defeated!

Triumph over Tragedy

In the hospital, Sheryl never complained about her disability and only expressed concerns about the unknown future she would face as a result of her stroke. She wondered about things she had previously taken for granted. One of the more important concerns she expressed was whether or not she would still be able to travel to countries around the world as she had done in the past. The good news is that since her stroke she has continued her travels to fantastic destinations like Hawaii, Portugal, Spain, Sweden, Africa, Mexico, Australia, and China, though she still needs her wheelchair to get around!

One of life's greatest tragedies is when any of us give up when we are actually closer than we'll ever know to achieving our goals.

On one of our more exotic trips, we traveled to Beijing, China, where we hoped to visit the Great Wall. We arranged to have a private tour guide take us to a small village at the base of a mountain nearby. We arrived in a small town in middle of a valley, but there was no Great Wall to be seen. I had visions that it would be like a Disney Ride that you could pull right up to and get on. As it turns out, the Great Wall was on top of the mountain, requiring a lengthy hike straight uphill!

The road leading up the mountain was made from primitive irregular cobblestone, and hard as we tried, we were only able to progress a short distance with Sheryl's wheelchair; she was being jarred severely every step of the way. It was clear that it would not be possible to push her up that mountain, and there was no way she could walk straight uphill for more than a mile. We had traveled half way around the world to see the Great Wall and it appeared there was no way for us to climb that final mountain to reach the summit!

Sheryl suggested I go ahead and hike up to see the Great Wall, take some pictures, and return. I refused to go. Ever since Sheryl had her stroke, I made a commitment to myself that if she is unable to do something, I wouldn't do it either. As much as we both wanted to see the Great Wall, there didn't seem to be a solution, until we noticed there were rickshaws for hire in the small town.

We approached one of the rickshaw owners and asked him, through an interpreter if he would be willing to pull Sheryl up the mountain. He said that he could do it if we were willing to pay two of his friends to push the rickshaw from behind as he pulled it! We negotiated a price; Sheryl got onboard, they loaded her wheelchair across the pull handles, and we were on our way up that mountain for a trip we will never forget. I can still picture Sheryl, riding like royalty in that rickshaw, being pushed and pulled all the way to the top! When we got close to what we thought was the summit, there was no Great Wall. Our destination was at an even higher elevation and the only way to get there was by taking a Swiss Alps style *"cable"* car. The problem we encountered next was how to get her to the cable car platform, which was three stories above us, up a

There are more than 7 billion people in the world, and every one of them faces adversity in their lives!

series of steep stone steps, which would be impossible for Sheryl to climb.

Again, we used good old-fashioned ingenuity. Sheryl got out of the rickshaw and into her wheelchair. Each of the Chinese rickshaw guys grabbed a corner of her wheelchair, and I grabbed the fourth corner, and together, we carried her up those three flights of stairs to the cable car platform! We boarded and rode that cable car all the way up to the summit. Though it wasn't easy, we reached our goal of visiting the Great Wall of China together!

As in this example, when you have high expectations, you can achieve almost any goal you set for yourself. It often helps to have some creative ideas along the way to solve the inevitable problems you will face. As in Sheryl's case, where there is a will, there is always a way to reach the summit. You too have the ability to reach the small and large goals you set for your life. Sometimes, those goals will seem out of reach, but those are the best kind! Stretch and you will usually achieve more than you ever thought was possible. Regardless of the challenges you face, stay positive, think creatively, and you will ultimately find a solution. Most importantly, never lose faith in your own ability to persevere.

At the end of my speech in Melbourne, Australia, I told the uplifting story of Sheryl's triumphant visit to the Great Wall of China, and then I delivered the following inspirational verse, *When Things Go Wrong,* by an unknown author that captures Sheryl's triumph over tragedy in an inspirational way.

When things go wrong as they sometimes will,
When the path you're walking seems all uphill,

When the funds are low and the debts are high,
And you want to smile, but you seem to sigh,

When care is pressing you down a bit,
Rest, if you must, but don't you quit.

Life seems strange with its twists and turns
Yet everyone of us eventually learns

That many a failure would turn about,
And you could have won had you stuck it out.

Don't give up though your pace seems slow -
You might succeed with just one more blow.

Often the goal is much nearer than
It might seem to a faltering woman or man.

You see often the victor has given up
When they might have captured the winners cup.

To later learn as the night slips down,
How close they were to the winners crown.

Success is failure turned inside out,
It's the silver tint of the clouds of doubt.

And you never can tell how close you are.
It may be near when it seems so far.

So stick to the fight when you're the hardest hit,
It's when things seem the worst that you mustn't quit.

Since Sheryl was in attendance in Melbourne that day, I decided to introduce her to the audience. I asked Sheryl, who was sitting in her wheelchair in the front row of the auditorium, to join me at the front of the stage. Since she arrived that day in her wheelchair, the audience had never seen her walk. They were quite shocked and surprised when she stood up, and by using her cane, was able to walk the short distance to where I was standing. In many ways, her walk to the stage that day symbolized how

You can bring out the best in others, if you'll start by bringing out the best in YOU!

she truly had triumphed over tragedy. Sheryl had survived a stroke, 10 days in a coma, 6 weeks recovering in a hospital, endured speech therapy, and ten years of physical therapy. Though she is still paralyzed on the right side of her body, she projects an attitude of gratitude, because she's thankful just to be alive, and it shows! There may be some things she can no longer do, but she can still do the important things in life. She is able to share the joy of reading a book, watch a movie with her family, groom her dog, care for her garden, talk to her friends on the telephone, decorate for the holidays, and experience the joy of traveling around the world. She has learned to laugh at things she once found stressful, found satisfaction in her accomplishments each day, lost focus on material things, and started living each day to its fullest knowing the uncertainty of tomorrow. She was given the rare gift of a second chance in life, and she intends to capitalize upon that opportunity; no disability is going to hold her back. Though circumstances outside her control forced her to experience the physical and emotional valleys in life, with high expectations, discipline, and a positive outlook she has chosen to persevere to become the best she can be, focused on her dreams, as she remains determined to reach life's summit.

As I handed her the microphone, I asked Sheryl, *"Is there anything you'd like to say to everyone here today?"* Gazing out at that audience with a defiant look on her face and tears in her eyes, Sheryl shared just two powerful and inspirational words of advice when she said,

"Don't Quit!"

APPENDIX

A TRIBUTE TO MY MENTORS

The following is a list of my personal mentors who made a difference in my life:

Michael's Mentors Lessons they taught me about life, living and business:

Sheryl Bergdahl *Don't focus on what you can't do, focus on what you can do.*

Robert Bergdahl Sr *The most important skill is the ability to present your ideas to others.*

Ginger Bergdahl *Being a writer allows your thoughts and ideas to influence others.*

Rachel Autio *No matter what you do, strive to be the best.*

Heather Bergdahl *Set aggressive personal standards that others aspire to reach.*

Paul Bergdahl *If you are willing to work hard, you can overcome any adversity.*

Joan Thomas *Don't be afraid to lean on others for emotional support in tough times.*

Craig Thomas *Trust in your own capability; try to do what you've never done before.*

Helen DeYoung *Successful entrepreneurs are tough, fair, smart, and decisive.*

Tom Burke *Write about things you know, like the stories of your life.*

Cil Clemente *Find your unique niche and you can make a difference in the world.*

Frank X. Maguire *Don't ever forget, the best is yet to come.*

Bill Gove *Make a point and tell a story, or tell a story and make a point.*

Jack Boget *Tell your audiences great stories and they'll never forget you.*

John Fisher *A few really good friends are important to happiness in life.*

Bill Meacci *Lead by your own example by setting the standard for your peers.*

Jim Withers *Find a way to pursue the dream God planted in your heart.*

Walter Fort *Disability is in the minds of others; choose to be enabled.*

Gary Brown *The human spirit always endures, even when the body comes under attack.*

Doug Lipp *Keep a healthy balance between your work life and your family life.*

Somers White *Speaking is the narrowest slice of your time; spend the rest marketing.*

Peter Garber *To complete a book, simply write a single page each day for 6 months.*

Ellen Fort Sometimes you must let people make mistakes for them to learn.

Jerry DeFalco *Don't make excuses, and don't accept excuses from others.*

Ruth Ann Butters *Some days there won't be a song in your heart, but caregivers sing anyway.*

Dr. Thomas Carmen *Even when you are busy, take time out to really listen to people.*

Delton Perkins *Don't allow others to keep you from pursuing your dreams.*

Joe Kerin *Sometimes you need to embrace those you perceive as your enemy.*

Dave Loeser *First impressions are critical to success in this world.*

Dave Werthman *You choose your own attitude each day. Make it a good one.*

Sam DeShazo *Invest as much energy in your family as you invest in your work.*

Sam Fleishman *Design and write marketable books with a targeted reader in mind.*

Sam Forman *Decision making in a business turnaround is not a democratic process.*

Sam Deep *To make a living giving paid speeches, you've got to write a book.*

Jim Nieves *It's better to set the bar high and miss than to set it low and achieve.*

Sam Walton *Believe in others even when they lack confidence in themselves.*

SHERYL'S ACKNOWLEDGEMENTS

Jodi and John Physical Therapists at Mercy Hospital

Ben Cole Physical Therapist who taught Sheryl to walk again

Brad Ciccolella Physical Therapist at NovaCare

Mickie Brown Lifelong Friend

Cil Clemente Deaf Education Teacher & Friend

Patty Cramer Lifelong Friend

Ellen Fort American Sign Language Interpreter, Teacher & Friend

Greg Jockel A Family Friend

MICHAEL BERGDAHL

His Background: Michael Bergdahl is a professional international business speaker, author and turnaround specialist. Bergdahl worked in Bentonville, Arkansas for Walmart, as the Director of "People" for the headquarters office. Previous to Walmart he worked in the FMCG Industry for PepsiCo's Frito-Lay Division in the sales organization and headquarters staff assignments. He is also a turnaround specialist who participated in two successful business turnarounds as a VP of HR at American Eagle Outfitters, and Waste Management. Bergdahl received the Senior Professional in Human Resources (SPHR) lifetime certification from SHRM. Bergdahl is a graduate of Penn State University with a Bachelor's Degree in Behavioral Science.

www.michaelbergdahl.net

SHERYL BERGDAHL

A graduate of the Pennsylvania State University, Sheryl was awarded a Bachelor of Arts Degree in Social Welfare. Sheryl is the mother of two children, Heather and Paul. Professionally, she has been a teacher and social worker, and she helps her husband, Michael, run his professional speaking business. Apart from her extensive travels in the United States, her business travels have taken her to five continents — North America, Asia, Australia, Europe, and Africa. When she is not engaged in her professional activities, Sheryl enjoys gardening on the Bergdahl farm in the hills of Western Pennsylvania. She is a self-professed tree hugger who loves the outdoors and all of nature's creatures!

High Expectations Are The Key To Everything is her first book.

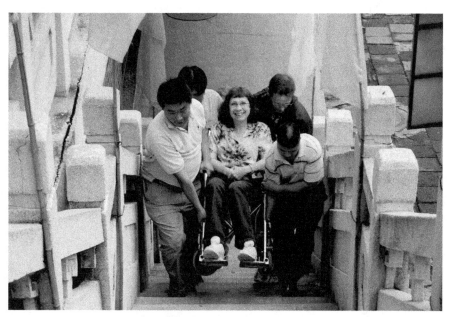

Sheryl and Michael Bergdahl at the Great Wall of China
High Expectations Are The Key To Everything!

CPSIA information can be obtained
at www.ICGtesting.com
Printed in the USA
BVHW031435311018
531730BV00005B/17/P

9 781628 650808